LEVISHAM:
a case study in Local History

Illustrations

	Page
Prehistoric tools	19
10th century gravestone	25
Chancel arch	33
12th century gravestone	42
Page from Levisham Court Book	47
Pickering Castle	49
Font	67
Page from Hearth Tax list	77
Cooking pot	83
St Mary's Church	95
Green Cottage	105
Plan of Levisham School	115
School Board Poster	124
Page from George Dixon's School Book	126
Emigrant Ship	127
Quebec Poster	137
Walker's Pit diagrams	139

The drawings on the chapter heading pages for chapters 2, 3, 4, 5, 7, 9, 10 & 11 are all by Doreen Crawley; for chapter 13 by Peter Halse.

Cover: Part of 17th century map of Pickering *Duchy of Lancaster copyright material in PRO*, reproduced by permission of the Chancellor and Council of the Duchy of Lancaster.

Aerial Photographs

Levisham from the air	7
Prehistoric settlements on Levisham Moor	22
Monastic Sheep Farm on Levisham Moor	59

Acknowledgements

This book owes its origins to the local history group that met first in Levisham in 1993. It has been brought to completion with the help of many people, particularly to Rosalin Barker and members of the Whitby Research Group who have read and advised on sections of the text; also to Graham Lee (National Parks Archaeologist) for guidance on the archaeology, and to John Harrison of the Cleveland Industrial and Archaeological Society for comments on the chapter on the iron industry.

I also wish to thank the National Park Authority and the Yorkshire Architectural and York Archaeological Society for financial help towards printing costs.

Contents

		Page
Introduction	Local History Today	1
Chapter 1	The Lie of the Land	7
Chapter 2	Humps and Bumps. *The time before written records*	19
Chapter 3	Dark Ages. *What can be known about the Anglo-Saxon period?*	25
Chapter 4	Under New Management. *How things were organised after the Conquest*	33
Chapter 5	Forest and Forest Law.	49
Chapter 6	Monks as Farmers.	59
Chapter 7	"William Watson, my Curate". *The role of church and priest in village life 1066-1700*	67
Chapter 8	Thomas Sowerby, Constable. *Looking after parish affairs 16th - 19th centuries*	77
Chapter 9	Three Centuries of Yeoman Farmers. *16th - 18th centuries*	83
Chapter 10	Isaac Wykes and Robert Skelton. *Village parsons in the 18th and 19th centuries*	95
Chapter 11	Enclosure and After. *Farming 18th and 19th centuries*	105
Chapter 12	Village School.	115
Chapter 13	On the Breadline. *Rural poverty in the 19th century*	127
Chapter 14	Walker's Pit. *A failed attempt at ironstone mining*	139

Maps

The maps of Levisham parish are all based on the 1848 Tithe Map.

The North York Moors: the area covered in this book	ii
The Lie of the Land: the physical features of Levisham	10
Routes: some of the early tracks connecting Levisham with its neighbours	12
Map of the projected Whitby - Pickering Canal	15
The Whitby - Pickering Canal	18
Archaeology: an indication of some of the archaeological sites on Levisham Moor	22
Castles: the string of castles along the southern edge of the moors between Scarborough and Helmsley	37
The Layout of Levisham: possibly a 12th century planned village	41
Bolebec's Levisham: an attempted reconstruction	43
The Royal Forest of Pickering	51
Monastic Houses with an approximate 20-mile radius of Levisham	62
Levisham after the 1770 Enclosure	108

Copyright: Betty Halse 2003

ISBN No: 0-9530717-1-5

Published by
Moors Publications
Levisham

Designed and printed@maxiprint.co.uk

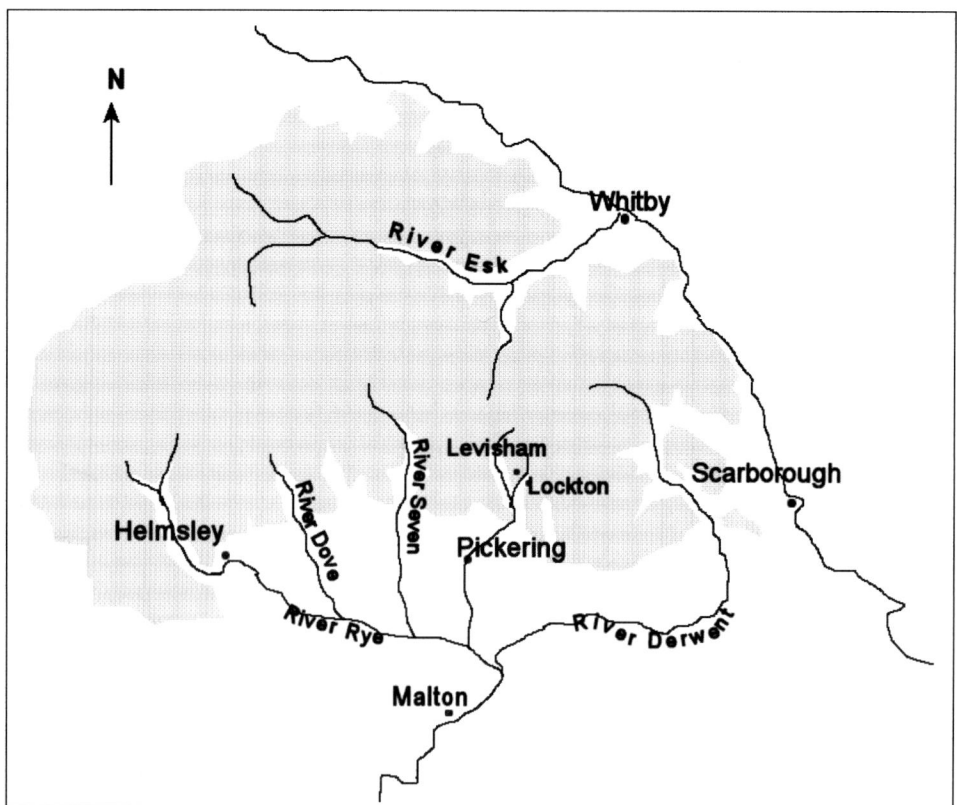

The North York Moors: the area covered in this book

Introduction

Local History Today

'The business of the local historian…is to re-enact in his own mind and to portray for his readers the Origin, Growth, Decline and Fall of a Local Community' (H.R.P. Finberg[1])

In the last half-century, local history has emerged from the dim and dusty recesses of the antiquarian's shelves to become a field of study that is recognised as a legitimate and distinct branch of history. Two landmarks in this process were the establishment of the first University Department of Local History at Leicester in 1947 and the formation of the Cambridge Group for the History of Population and Social Structure in 1964. Today, there are courses and classes in local history going on everywhere from university lecture rooms to village halls; there are Local History societies and groups to join, and a huge quantity of literature ranging from the erudite to the popular to stimulate and inform those with an interest in the subject. What is more, amateurs – enthusiasts, with local knowledge and willingness to work in a disciplined way, – are recognised as essential partners in the work of collecting, recording and interpreting local historical data. Local historians are offered both an opportunity and a challenge.

In this new climate, some very basic questions about the nature and content of the subject are under active discussion: what *is* 'local history'? What are its objectives? What is its relationship to national and international history? Is there an appropriate framework that can help us to develop our understanding of local communities?[2]

Local history is seen as a branch of social history, its key questions centring round the everyday lives and concerns of ordinary citizens. It

---

[1] Finberg p.9   [2] Finberg & Tripp: Local History

is concerned with 'the small print of history'[3] It is narrow-focus history, working with a microscope rather than a telescope,[4] looking at the small-scale and particular set within the context of the wide sweep of general cultural trends, of international and national events. It is, at the same time, broad in its range, taking in a number of specialist areas each with its own methods and discipline – for example archaeology, vernacular architecture, demography, family reconstruction. No individual is likely to have expertise to deal with everything; everyone can discover where to find the experts.

Local history is, by definition, linked to a particular place – a village, town, or region. Where are the boundaries to be drawn? If a village community is the object of study, it is not satisfactory to draw a hard line round the parish boundary, making that the limit of the enquiry. 'No man is an island', and neither is any local community. The inhabitants of the village are, and have always been, part of other networks: they are members of families, which may be geographically widespread; they have work connections; religious affiliations. Everyone has civic obligations extending beyond the parish – taxes to pay, laws to obey (or suffer the consequences). One particular local community cannot be viewed simply as 'a society': it is composed of a number of inter-related societies.[5] The scope of local history has to be wide enough to take into its awareness these overlapping circles that spread out from the centre that is the focus of the study; it must attempt to map the communication links that tie a community into its wider world. It is a study in 'human ecology',[6] its field of interest all the people, not just those of a particular class, all that goes on, not just special events. It is the run-of-the-mill-rather than the remarkable, the usual rather than the unusual, that concerns the local historian.

The locality, the place that provides its primary focus, is where local historians find their starting point. One of the attractions of local history to the inexperienced researcher is its accessibility. The place itself is there, at hand, clues to its past all around. Some at least of the

---

[3] Rosalin Barker

[4] W.G.Hoskins: English Local History: Past and Future

[5] Charles Pythian-Adams

[6] Hoskins: op.cit.

documentary records will be readily available in local libraries and museums and the County Record Office. There will be people who have old photographs and other relics from the past, people whose memories can be recorded. It may be some local feature – a house, the church, farm buildings, or perhaps an old map or photographs that sparks the initial interest, provoking the question that becomes the first step on what turns out to be a fascinating and never-ending trail.

A Local History Project

This book is written for people involved, either individually or in a group, in some kind of Local History project – or for anyone who would like to set about such a project but feels uncertain about how to start. The concept of a 'project', defined as *'an individual or collaborative enterprise …', 'a usually long-term exercise or study of a topic undertaken by (*an individual) *or group…'* [7] can be useful in steering the researcher towards a manageable, clearly defined piece of work with a definite end-product. It is all too easy to go on collecting information until you get lost in a jungle of paper! A small, specific undertaking concentrates the mind, and will inevitably open up avenues for future exploration.

The way a project can develop, change, branch out in different directions can be illustrated from work done in Levisham. We started with an informal group meeting over the course of one winter with the vague and generalised aim of seeing what could be discovered about the history of the village; soon we settled down to focus on the eighteenth and nineteenth centuries – the easiest period to start with as there is such an abundance of readily accessible documentary material. Quickly, several subsidiary projects emerged, undertaken by different members of the group. One major task was the transcription and putting onto computer of various key documents – Parish Registers, Census Returns, the Enclosure Award, the Tithe Award schedule – so that they could be available for the whole group to work on. The monumental inscriptions in the Churchyard were recorded; photographs of the village, past and present, collected. The winter's

[7] OED

work culminated in an exhibition in the Village Hall in 1993 which stimulated more interest and brought in additional material. Everything that had been collected formed the beginning of a further on-going project – the creation of a Village Archive.

And so it goes on…

The Process of doing Local History

A historian is trying to reconstruct and understand something that no longer exists. The past is gone, but is worth investigating because it provides a context, a framework of interpretation to help us understand the present. History provides the thread of continuity running through a process of continual change.

A piece of historical investigation has to be based on something that dates from the period under review – a 'primary source', which may be a document, a building, an artefact, a reminiscence. The researcher needs to keep going back to the primary sources, continually checking, continually questioning them. The fact that a source is 'primary' or 'original' does not guarantee its accuracy. Even official documents such as Census Returns or Parish Registers are sometimes wrong: people make mistakes or can occasionally intend to mislead. Questions need to be asked about the purpose for which a document or official record was produced, and who produced it. As will be noticed later, Domesday Book records very few churches in North Yorkshire: was this because they did not exist, or because of the dislocation caused by the 'harrying of the north' – or was there some other reason? When people's names are known from official documents, we shall for most of recorded history meet mainly men, and our acquaintance will be with the well-to-do who paid taxes and held official positions. A woman is only likely to appear if a widow, or the mother of a minor – like the 'Domina' or 'Lady' of Levisham Scolastica, widow of Godfrey de Melsa named in tax returns of 1327 when she was acting for her young son John.

The investigation will also be likely to involve reading what other historians have written – 'secondary sources'. Any statement in a secondary source should be capable of verification by reference to the primary source that is behind it. A sceptical attitude needs to be cultivated, a state of mind that accepts nothing without asking 'what is the evidence…?'

Sources provide the material to work on, but offer no instant answers, no ready-made 'story'. The process of bringing history to life, making a narrative out of a series of events, requires the exercise of imagination – not in the flight-of-fancy sense that turns history into romantic fiction, but in order to make connections, to envisage different possible interpretations of evidence, to formulate the questions that need addressing to the evidence in order to take the investigation further.

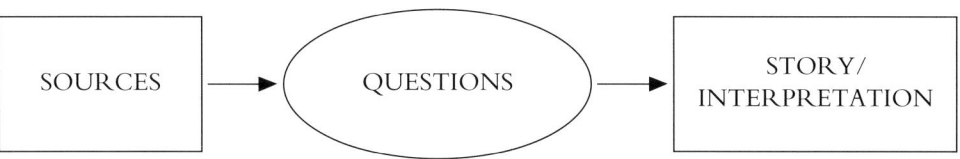

Keeping Records

Before getting in too deep, decisions need to be made about how work is to be recorded. What starts in a notebook can soon grow into a paper jungle, where valuable treasures are lost in the undergrowth.

Whether the system is A4 folders, card index, computer or a combination of all three it needs to be carefully thought out before starting. Is the filing system to be organised by chronology or topics? Is there a method of cross-referencing? Where is it all to be kept?

A computer is an invaluable tool for storage, organisation and reproduction of material. A relational database that enables cross-referencing between different tables can be particularly useful, but requires before setting it up a clear idea both of the kind of information to be stored and the use that is to be made of it.

As part of the record keeping, make a note of all sources of information whether from a book, document, place or person. Keep full details of book references – publisher, page reference, where the book can be found; who knows when it may need to be consulted again? Similarly with photographs or maps: note details of place, date, and where the original can be found.

End Product

To have an end product in view helps to focus the mind. The amassing of information can be an engrossing occupation following one trail after another, filling file after file with interesting data. At some point a decision must be made about how this material can be shaped into some coherent form. In the process, much will be discarded or left unused, but the finished presentation should aim to make accessible to other people what has been researched. Computers have transformed the possibilities here, making it easy to produce small-scale illustrated publications on a DIY basis.

This book is an attempt both to clarify the process of working on local history and to illustrate it from the history of the village of Levisham.

Each chapter follows the same pattern:
- **CHRONOLOGY–** a chart of some relevant dates to act as anchor points
- **SOURCES -** a chart listing sources useful for local historians in this area, followed by explanation of what they are, where they can be found, how they can be used
- **BACKGROUND** - information to put the theme of the chapter into its context;
- **LEVISHAM -** one aspect of the history of the village of Levisham, presented as a case-study, illustrating how available sources can be used to develop an understanding of a particular historical theme.

The book makes no attempt to be comprehensive. It is full of loose ends.

There is nothing in it that could not be discovered by any local historian with the interest and time to spend on the search.

These are books specially recommended for their readability, and the insight they provide for the general reader.

Chapter 1: The Lie of the Land

'The English landscape itself, to those who know how to read it right, is the richest historical record we possess' W. G. Hoskins

Levisham from the air surrounded by its arable fields, with the two lanes leading north onto the moor, and the steep valley to the south and east separating it from the neighbouring village of Lockton © North Yorkshire County Council

CHRONOLOGY

Geological times

213million – 150million years ago	rocks of N.York Moors deposited as sediment under sea
65million years ago	area uplifted to form land
2million years ago	onset of last Ice Age
10,000 years ago	melt water from Eskdale carved out Newtondale
8000-4500 BC	evidence of human activity on North York Moors

Historic times

Bronze Age c.1700-600 BC	Clearing of forests. Beginning of agriculture. Boundary dykes.
Iron Age c.600 BC – 70 AD	Expansion of farming with improved technology.
Roman era 70 – 410 AD	Roads. Military and civilian settlements.
Anglo-Saxons 6th – 11th C	Nucleated settlements. Open-field farming.
Medieval	Royal Forest. Monastic estates.
18th – 19th C	Enclosures: changed field patterns; walls and hedges. Turnpike roads: 1764 Whitby - Lockton Canals: 1793-4 proposed Whitby – Pickering canal Railways: 1836 Whitby – Pickering line opened.

SOURCES

On the ground	Documentary
The landscape: walking boots needed!	Maps Aerial photographs Enclosure and Tithe Awards

The history of any community is rooted in its landscape. Why was a settlement made in that place? How and why did it develop in the way it did? How were its boundaries defined? What were its lines of communication with its neighbours, and to the wider world beyond? Answers to questions like these reach back into its geology, and to its geographical situation. The development of any place is related to its accessibility by land or water, to factors such as the type and quality of the soil, to mineral deposits.

The underlying features of the landscape arise from the geological formation of the land hundreds of millions of years ago and to the effects of climatic changes over long periods of time before the emergence of human life. Human activity has continued the process of change ever since. The landscape we know today has been created by the farmers, miners, industrialists, sportsmen – everyone who over the centuries has cleared forests, ploughed the earth, laid out fields, quarried stone and built with it, made roads and bridges – all the human activities that make use of the resources of nature and which leave the environment in some way altered. A practiced eye can 'read' a landscape and discover from it some of the factors that have shaped the history of the area.

The primary need for the foundation of any settlement is food, from land, river or sea. The nature of the soil determines the type of agriculture that is possible, what crops will thrive, whether it is sheep or cattle country.

Buildings differ from one locality to another according to the available stone, timber, thatching material. Even demographic patterns of marriages and births are related to the land, depending on the seasonal occupations of the particular community, different for people living from the sea from those living from the land; differing in areas where the busiest season of the year is the grain harvest from those whose greatest pressure comes in the spring at lambing time.

The earliest trackways were beaten by feet tramping from house to field, from village to village, from the place of production to market. Such routes grew up, as it were, organically, arising out of the daily life of the people who used them, following the contours, avoiding boggy valley bottoms, crossing streams where they could be forded or bridged. Romans roads were made in a different manner, engineered roads to serve one specific purpose, no expense spared. Monks created tracks to link a mother house with its daughter houses and its outlying granges, or to get their wool to its collection points. Towns that grew up round castles needed good communication with other administrative centres, while the ever increasing traffic of trade led to the creation of paved pannier-ways across the moors that could be used by pack-horses.

For centuries, the maintenance of roads and bridges was the duty of each parish, dependent on the availability of local materials and local ox, horse and manpower. By the eighteenth century, transport needs required more ambitious planning, while new technologies opened up new possibilities. Turnpike roads were constructed for use by coaches, financed by profit-making Trusts deriving their income from tolls paid by the users. Canals linked the sea to centres of trade, and made connections between navigable rivers. With the nineteenth

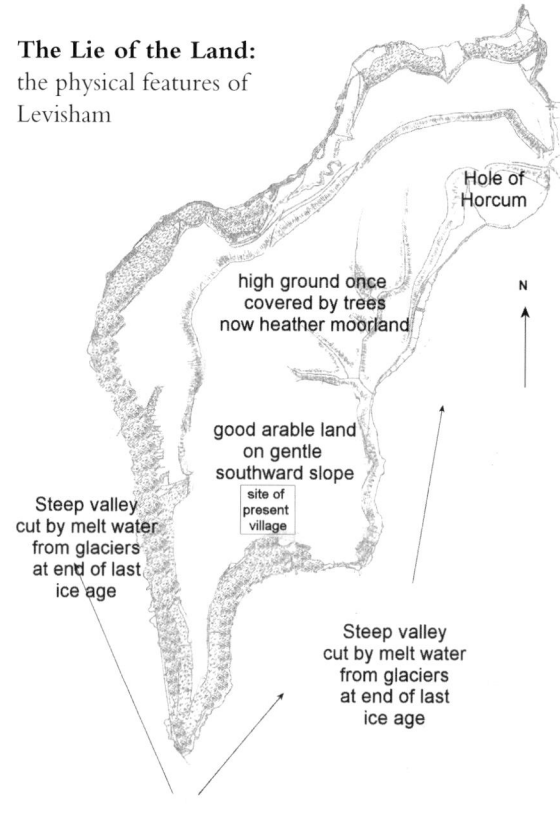

The Lie of the Land: the physical features of Levisham

century, railways revolutionised both passenger and goods transport, opening up the country in a new way – to be superseded in the following century by the petrol-driven car and lorry, leading to the building of the network of motorways and roads we are familiar with today. And behind all this activity, the surveyor studying the terrain, his work dependent on rock formations, gradients, water courses: the lie of the land.

Levisham

Levisham is situated on the edge of the North York Moors, 200 feet above sea level. It lies 6 miles north of Pickering on the south-facing slope of the Tabular Hills as they drop down into the Vale of Pickering. It can be reached from three directions - on foot across the moors from the north, or by narrow, winding roads that climb up from the steep-sided valleys that form the parish boundaries to the south east and south west. Of the 3000 acres of land within the parish, two thirds is moorland. There are around 500 acres of arable land on limestone soil.

The landscape we know today has not always been there. Landscape has its own history that goes back long before the advent of human beings and which has a permanent influence on all subsequent human history. A plough working the arable fields of Levisham sometimes turns up an ammonite, or a hunk of fossilized shells, indicating that what is now a field was once under the sea, before the violent movements of the earth's crust that lifted and tilted the layers of rock deposited under the sea, settling the land into its present contours.

What we know today as heather moorland was once covered with trees. The change came about through a combination of forest clearance by Bronze Age farmers together with a climate shift to colder conditions. The heather was encouraged to serve the needs of grouse-shooting sportsmen in the nineteenth century.

Iron deposits beneath the moor were worked during the middle ages when there are records of payments for the right to have an iron forge, and fines for cutting down wood to make charcoal. In the nineteenth century, an unsuccessful attempt was made to develop an iron works in Newtondale; the iron proved to be not of sufficient quality or quantity to be commercially viable.

In this bleak, upland area, cut by steep valleys carved out by the melting of glaciers, communications must always have been difficult. Wayfarers making their way across the lonely tracts of moorland would have been glad of the stone crosses erected at strategic points as waymarkers. Today, many of the old tracks have become submerged in forestry plantations or other new land uses. Some can still be traced; some are used as public footpaths, where a walker may become aware of ancient flagstones that mark it as a 'trod', a way paved to carry the traffic of monks or panniermen centuries ago. In some places, a stretch of an old 'holloway' survives, sunk between ancient banks. Old maps

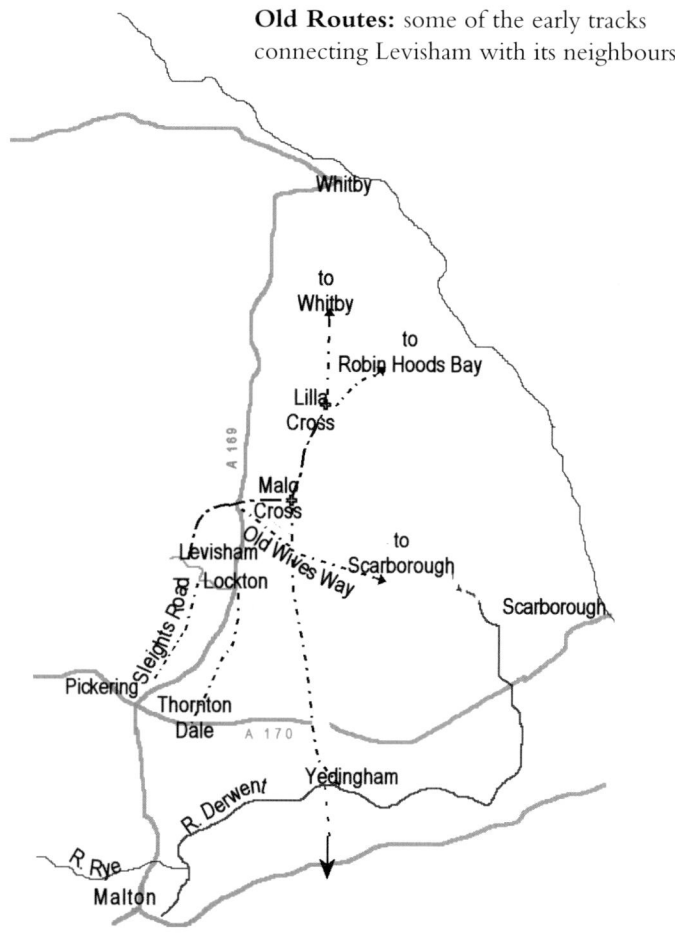

Old Routes: some of the early tracks connecting Levisham with its neighbours

of the area round Levisham show a network of tracks quite different from today's road system.[1]

In Levisham, the mains street through the village was often referred to in eighteenth century deeds as 'King Street' – that is, the 'King's Highway', a road required to be maintained by the parish. It leads out of the village to the north by way of two lanes, Braygate and Limpseygate, both documented as far back as the thirteenth century. They emerge onto the moor, where a track heads across to Saltersgate. Here the traveller could either turn east along the Old Wives Way or Trod, a pack-horse road following Crosscliff Brow to Bickely, Hackness, and on to the coast at Scarborough, or take a track heading north along Saltergate Brow. After dropping down to Malo Cross, and a trek around May Moss, another waymarker, Lilla Cross, signed the point where tracks diverged to Robin Hood's Bay or Whitby. The names of these crosses commemorate local personalities: Malo, like Mauley Cross a few miles to the west, both called after the Mauley family of Mulgrave Castle, Lilla Cross said to mark the grave of the hero who in the seventh century lost his own life in saving his king, Edwin of Northumbria, from assassination.

The name 'Saltersgate' is a reminder of the importance of the trade in salt, the essential food preservative, brought along these tracks from the salterns (where brine from sea water was evaporated to produced salt) on the coast to markets inland. Another of the tracks across the moor is shown on some maps as the 'Lime Road', used for carting limestone to be used for fertiliser from quarries like those to the north east of Lockton, a trade that was discontinued when lime was brought in more cheaply by sea to Whitby in the late eighteenth century.[2]

Leaving Levisham to the south, the way down the hill towards Lockton passed St Mary's Church, crossed the beck, and met a track still marked on maps as 'Sleights Road', heading towards Pickering along the hillside well above the level of the marshy valley bottom, still a very clearly defined cart-track.

---

[1] Warburton 1720; Greenwood 1818; Knox 1849

[2] It has been suggested that the name 'Limpseygate Lane' derives from its use as a lime road

Streams and rivers have a bearing on the course of a road, both on account of the need to avoid swamps and possible flooding, and the need to find suitable crossing places. Howe Bridge, between Pickering and Malton, and a bridge at Yedingham were crossing-points of the river Rye for two main north-south routes, the Yedingham bridge (originally at Foulbridge where the Knights Templar had a house) on the main route south from Whitby Abbey.[3]

When, in the eighteenth century, improved transport was recognised as part of the necessary infrastructure for economic development, local business people began to plan the building of a new Turnpike road south from Whitby. Until this time Whitby, with its excellent harbour and flourishing sea-borne trade, had been a difficult place to reach overland, its access roads *'in a state of nature, rough, rugged and uneven'*.[4] The petition to Parliament preceding the Turnpike Act referred to *'miry deep lanes'*, *'wide open boggy moors'*, with the danger of travellers getting lost or stuck. From 1759, subscriptions were being collected towards the project. A Turnpike Act of 1764 sanctioned the construction of the road from Sleights to Lockton lane end; the following year of an additional Act covered the extension of the road from Lockton to Pickering. This was a completely new road, not following the line of former tracks, but built right over the top of the moor. Regular stage and mail coaches were in service along the road by the late 1780's. Tuke, in his survey of Agriculture in the North Riding published in 1800, considered the road to have been badly planned, with eight miles of *'continued steep ascent or descent'* which might have been avoided.[5] He recognised that the inadequacy of roads in the area was the result of both neglect, and ignorance of *'proper construction and management'*, and saw that improvement would require a readiness to spend money.

By this time, there were people looking seriously into ways of financing and developing better means of transport. Following the success of the Bridgewater Canal from Worsley to Manchester, canals caught the public imagination as a more efficient means of shipping

---

[3] see chapter 9 ed. Spratt & Harrison: Landscape History; map of medieval roads p.188

[4] Whitby historian Lionel Charlton c. 1776, quoted Macmahon 34

[5] Tuke p.301

goods round the country. A group of gentlemen from the Whitby-Pickering area headed by the Rt. Hon. Henry Earl Fauconberg formed a committee to promote the building of a canal along Newtondale from Whitby to Pickering. Here was a new way of looking at the landscape, seeing a deep valley not as a barrier but as a natural feature that could be utilised. Robert Skelton, Rector of Levisham, was one of the eighteen committee members who in 1793 commissioned William Crosley, *'an Engineer of great eminence'* to carry out a survey.[6] A copy of extracts from a report circulated to the committee gives an insight into their thinking and includes some of the calculations that gave them grounds for optimism.

They were inspired with the belief in progress, the possibility of bringing about improvement that was the aspiration of their age. The

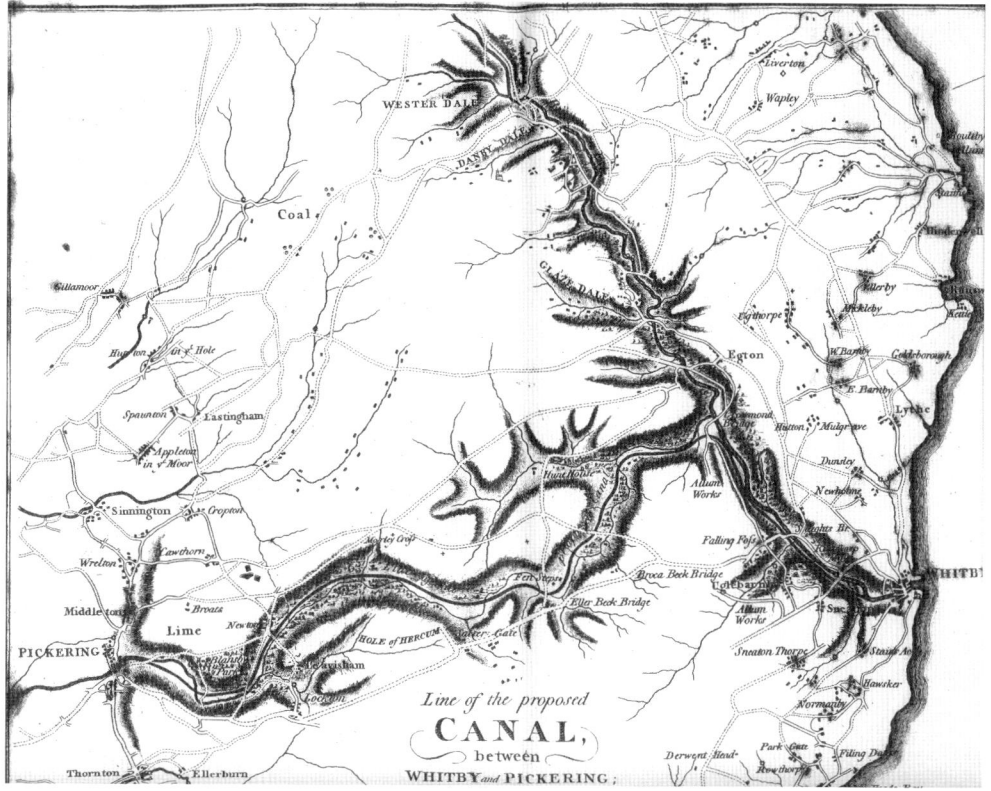

Map of the projected Whitby-Pickering Canal Courtesy Whitby Literary & Philosophical Society

[6] P.Burnett's Papers. X123 Whitby Lit. and Phil.

report takes as its text, as it were, a quotation from Dean Swift that *'the man who causes a single blade of grass to grow where none ever appeared before deserves more from society than all the politicians that have existed'*. They were envisaging the conversion of *'unprofitable wastes into cultivated fields'* and looked forward to being able to *'add real strength and riches to their country by increasing its population'*. They believed the canal would be able to bring to Whitby from the Pickering area grain, timber for boat-building, stone for piers and town buildings. It could take inland from Whitby lime brought down the coast from Sunderland at a cheaper price than farmers were currently paying, and other goods imported by sea. They proposed a weekly Market Boat carrying in one direction imported goods that would be marketable in Pickering, and returning laden with farm produce for Whitby consumption. They did their sums, and came to the conclusion that the investors whose money would be needed to pay the estimated £66,447 building costs could expect interest of five per cent.

The project never went ahead, but the work that had gone into its planning was not wasted. The possibilities of using Newtondale as a route for conveying goods between Whitby and Pickering was kept in mind, and re-emerged when railway technology developed. The need for inland routes to Whitby grew more acute as old industries – shipbuilding, whaling, alum mining – declined. When experimental work began on the Stockton-Darlington rail project, Whitby business-men were amongst the subscribers, and discussion began on the idea of a railway to Whitby. Different routes were canvassed. In 1832 George Stephenson was asked to look at the alternatives; his report favoured the route that had been surveyed for the canal – through the Esk valley to Grosmont, and from there via Goathland Dale into Newtondale. The steepest gradient to be negotiated was the rise into Goathland. When the line was opened in 1836, it had cost twice as much as the £80,000 that Stephenson had estimated. Horses were used to draw the coaches – stage coach bodies on railway wheels – a single horse capable of pulling two coaches for most of the route, a second horse needed for the long pull up between Raindale and Fen Bog. The horse was unyoked before the Beck Hole incline. Here, coaches were attached to a thick rope, (5 inches in diameter), which passed round a horizontal wheel at the top of the incline, its other end attached to a water tank. The preponderating weight of the descending tank raised the coaches. The tank was then emptied, and drawn up again, to be refilled from a reservoir ready for the next train. On downhill stretches, from Fen Bog to Levisham and between Grosmont and Whitby, the coaches were allowed to run down under their own momentum.

As railways proved their worth, it became clear that the Whitby to Pickering line needed to be connected to the fast developing national network, and negotiations were opened with 'Railway King' George Hudson. The Whitby and Pickering Railway was bought up by the Hudson's York and North Midland Company, and in 1847 the newly linked-up line to York was opened, using steam locomotives. Some reconstruction of the line had been needed – a larger tunnel at Goathland, a stone bridge at Grosmont, a stationary engine to work the hoist at the Beck Hole inclined plane. After a fatal accident here in 1864 when the rope broke, a section of the line between Beck Hole and Goathland was relocated.

The nature of its site has made Levisham for most of its history a very distinct, rather isolated community. Its economy has been based entirely on agriculture (predominantly sheep) until recent times. The railway made the village accessible for the first time to people from further afield: James Walker from Leeds coming to live at the Hall in the 1860's hoping to develop iron-stone mining; Barnes Wimbush from London in the 1890's to enjoy the sporting potential of Levisham Moor. Today, the railway's continued existence is for tourists, while holiday cottages and guest-houses meet the needs of visitors looking for space and leisure to enjoy the rugged beauty of the area. The landscape is as important as it ever was, but is viewed and valued from a different perspective.

The Floating Egg. Episodes in the Making of Geology. Roger Osborne (Pimlico 1999) *An unusual and fascinating book on the geology of north Yorkshire, making a sometimes obscure subject accessible to the non-expert.*

LEVISHAM: A CASE STUDY IN LOCAL HISTORY

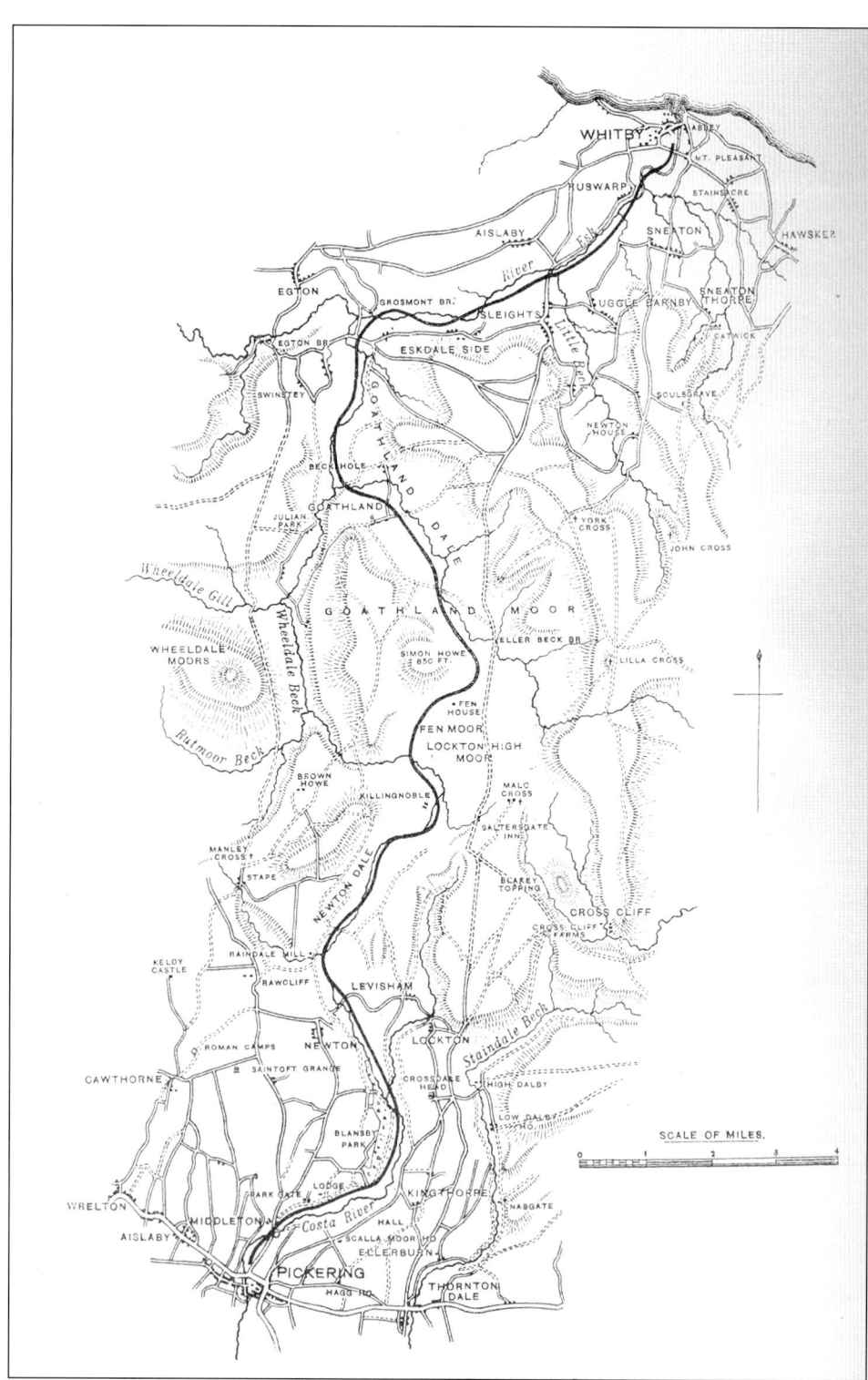

The Whitby-Pickering Railway from Tomlinson: N. Eastern Railway

Chapter 2:
Humps and Bumps
The time before written records

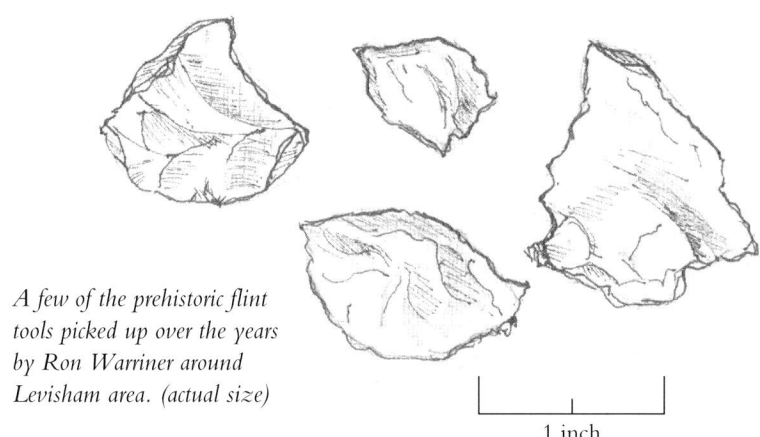

A few of the prehistoric flint tools picked up over the years by Ron Warriner around Levisham area. (actual size)

1 inch

CHRONOLOGY

Period	Finds in area of North York Moors	Interpretation
c.7600 – 3500 Mesolithic period	Stone hunting tools – scrapers, blade	Population of hunter-gatherers
c.3500 – 2500 BC Neolithic period	Tools for hunting and farming; pottery; long barrows for burials	Beginning of settled life & farming
c.2000 – 500 BC Bronze Age	Round barrow burials. Earthworks as territorial boundaries. Field systems	Increased population; forest clearance.
c.500 BC – 200 AD Iron Age	Enclosures, huts, field systems, pottery	Settled agricultural population

SOURCES

Archaeological sites	maps and interpretative books needed
Museums	

Where does history begin?

The natural place to begin, is at the beginning – but the beginning of history is just the part that is most obscure.

For the greater part of the 5,000 or so years that humans are known to have been around in this part of the world, there are no written records, no words. The only clues to the lives of these early ancestors come from what can be literally unearthed by archaeologists. We observe humps and bumps in the landscape or see from aerial photographs patterns that were clearly not made by nature, and know that people have been at work, building, fortifying, farming. Artefacts made from durable materials like stone, bone, metal, pottery give some indications of the life style and skills of their makers, whose names, identities, thoughts, beliefs are forever closed to us.

After observing, comparing, using some of the technology that now makes it possible to date and reconstruct the finds that have been made, there comes the task of interpretation: what do these finds tell us about the people and the culture to which they belonged?

The story the archaeologist tells is always provisional, always subject to revision as more finds come to light, new technology is developed, or different theories are advanced to make sense of the available evidence.

A century ago, archaeology tended to be a hobby of country gentlemen who went treasure hunting in an unsystematic way, often damaging or destroying the sites that they investigated. Today, archaeology has become a highly specialised area of study, and one that is outside the scope of this book. All that is attempted here is a little sketch of what the amateur local historian can observe and deduce, and an indication of where to look for further information.

The First People

Observant walkers with their eyes on the ground may sometimes come across small pieces of worked flint, carefully shaped to make tools and weapons – arrow-heads, spear points, knives, scrapers. They provide evidence that the area was populated during the Stone Ages (roughly 7000 – 3000 BC). Ron Warriner of Levisham, (whose grandfather's collection of similar stones is now in the York Museum), has over the years picked up a number of these Stone Age artefacts while walking around the Levisham area. As a practical countryman, he had no difficulty in envisaging how they were used: the scraper with its serrated edge, about 8cm across, fitting snugly into the palm of the hand of the hunter preparing to skin his rabbit; several similarly shaped but much smaller and finer cutting tools; the elongated pointed triangle of a spearhead, and a tiny, delicate razor-sharp arrowhead 1.5cm long.

Discovering early farming.

How to go about archaeological research can be illustrated from this account of how two local people investigated an area on Levisham Moor.

Edna and Derek King's interest in archaeology began in an evening class in York, and was developed through working with the York Archaeological Society. They learned some of the basic archaeological skills: how to observe a landscape with a discerning eye, and how to set about recording accurately what they saw.

Here is Edna's account of their recognition of a site of archaeological interest, and their systematic mapping of what they found:

In the 1960s, in light snow, we could see lines running across Rhumbard Snout which were invisible at other times of the year.

In the 1970s, the National Parks Authority sprayed the bracken on the moor and we began to see the lines more clearly. We realised that there were at least 7 lines running roughly parallel from east to west across the Snout, with cross walls in places and many little cairns in some of the fields thus formed.

We decided that this was worth recording and accordingly devised a system of layout in 150 yard squares with the footpath across the centre of the site as a rough datum line.

We made a large set-square to allow us to set the right angles and measured off 5 yard lengths along 2 coils of polypropylene rope marking each 5 yards with a yellow tape and every 20 yards with a red tape. This allowed us to invent a system of marker pegs at regular intervals across and down the site which we used as we recorded every rock on that moor! It took us most of 2 years...

The plan which they produced showed evidence of a series of terraces across the gently sloping south-facing area of ground. Now heather moorland, pollen analysis has shown that the whole area of the

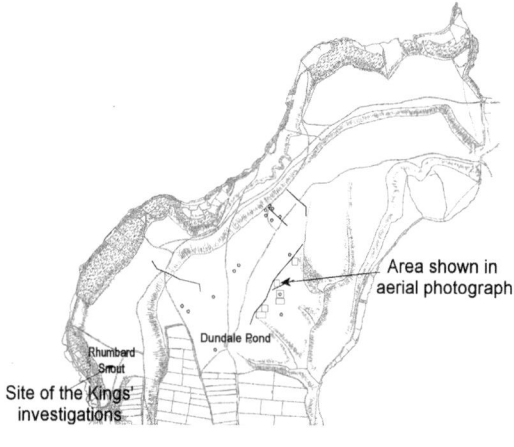

Archaeology: an indication of some of the archaeological sites on Levisham Moor

Iron Age Sites on Levisham Moor: some of the many pieces of evidence of prehistoric inhabitants, hard to observe on the ground but clearly visible in an aerial photograph. © Crown Copyright. NMR

moors was once covered by forest which, it is believed, was gradually cleared by farmers from the Bronze Age early practitioners of 'slash and burn' methods, (c.2000 years BC) onwards.[1] On Rhumbard Snout it seems possible that people from this early period cut down the trees and cleared the ground, using the stones they cleared to make walls or piling them up in cairns. There is at least one hut circle indicating where the farmers lived. The shallow earth, cultivated by primitive tools of wood or bronze, would produce crops for a few years when the trees were first cleared, but without fertilisers the farmers would then have to move on to find fresh land to cultivate.

On the higher level of Levisham Moor are more obvious indications of the presence of early inhabitants. There are a number of round burial mounds sited in prominent positions, believed to date from the Bronze Age, and a series of linear earthworks and ditches similar to those in other parts of North Yorkshire thought to be from a later date.

The presence of farmers from the Iron Age can be deduced from enclosures, dykes, hut circles found during archaeological work on Levisham Moor in the 1960's.[2] These include a very clearly defined small square enclosure sometimes referred to as the 'War Camp'. Was it a defensive position? Or was it, as another interpretation suggests, a stock enclosure constructed in the shape of a small Roman fort by people who had become familiar with Roman building styles? Interesting questions arise about the extent of Roman influence in Northern Britain. How much interaction was there between the military occupiers and their British subjects? The discovery of pieces of Roman roof and flue tiles and plaster from walls in debris on a site near Farwath,[3] as well as considerable Roman material from the site of a Roman villa on the edge of Blansby Park[4] near Pickering point to a larger Romanised civilian presence in this area than had at one time been suspected.

Within one of the identifiable Iron Age enclosures on Levisham Moor was found an iron bloomery which was assumed to belong to

---

[1] Atherden
[2] Prehistoric and Roman Archaeology of N.E.Yorkshire p.148
[3] N.E.Yorkshire Studies. Archaeological papers: R.H.Hayes. ed P.R.Wilson
[4] Ryedale Historian 2002

that same period. Recently, this dating has been questioned: the design of the furnace with a slag-tapping hole in the side suggest that it may date from medieval times when an iron forge is known to have been operating. Further investigation of the site is likely to bring clarification: archaeologists have continually to revise their interpretations of the past in the light of new knowledge.

All that has been discovered indicates that this area of heather moorland now tramped over by walkers and grazed by sheep, has over many centuries in the past supported a population large enough to construct extensive boundary earthworks; people who have left traces of field systems and hut circles, whose burial mounds stand out on the sky-line, but whose thinking and way of life we can only guess at.

Archaeology is the way in to discovering what can be known about these earliest periods of human history, before people left records of themselves in writing. Its methods are increasingly specialised and technical. Knowledge about climate change, methods of accurate dating, cross-referencing between different areas, all contribute to gaining a fuller and more accurate picture of these early forebears; but there will always be a great many unanswered questions, always more to be observed and explored, and always the possibility of new evidence being turned up to challenge established theories.

Chapter 3: Dark Ages

What can be known about the Anglo-Saxon period?

This 10th century grave slab carved with a mythical beast, now in the porch of the Parish Church, is evidence of a graveyard dating from the Anglo-Saxon period.

LEVISHAM: A CASE STUDY IN LOCAL HISTORY

CHRONOLOGY

Date	National	Local
410	Withdrawal of Roman army from Britain	
5th–7th C	Gradual incursion of Anglo-Saxon settlers	Anglian settlements in North Yorkshire
7th C		Foundation of kingdom of Northumbria
634-51		Aidan, Bishop of Lindisfarne's mission to convert Northumbria
657		Foundation of monastery at Whitby; monastery at Lastingham
664		Synod of Whitby
731	Bede's Ecclesiastical History of the English People	
8th – 9th C	Viking raids	Viking kingdom of York Whitby abbey destroyed in Viking raids
9thC	Alfred the Great Anglo-Saxon Chronicle compiled	

SOURCES

On the ground	Written
Some church masonry from Levisham in Ryedale Folk Museum	Place names (books about place names in all libraries)
Grave-slab from Viking period in Levisham Church porch	Chronicles and histories (Gildas mid-sixth century, Bede mid-eighth century).
Exhibition at Whitby Abbey Heritage Centre	Domesday Book
Museums	

The obscurity of this period is to do with the sparseness of the sources.

The Romans, literate and with sophisticated building, with their engineering and administrative skills, were succeeded by folk whose enduring legacy was in their settlements, customs and language. Their presence was not recorded in written words or impressive stone buildings. The accounts of their arrival in early histories by chroniclers like Gildas and Bede were written too long after the events they describe to be reliable, and apart from Bede, were written without regard for what we would consider a proper sense of historical evidence.

When settlements founded during this period have continued as villages or towns to the present day, as is usually the case, any archaeological trace of their origins is likely to lie buried deep below the modern streets and buildings. Early remains only emerge by chance when a new building development requires the excavation of a site, or through an event like the cliff fall in Whitby in the year 2000 which exposed evidence of an extensive town, hitherto unknown.

The study of place names gives useful pointers to the origins of early settlements, and has been extensively written about.

Domesday Book, compiled a generation after the Norman Conquest, refers back to how things were at the time of Edward the Confessor and so is a limited but useful source for the final period of Anglo-Saxon England.

Background

The withdrawal of the Roman army after 400 years of occupation left Britain exposed to increasingly frequent incursions of peoples of Germanic origin. There is no contemporary record of these Anglo-Saxon invasions. Oral traditions were written down at a later date, providing stories which archaeologists attempt to find evidence to corroborate. The picture given by Bede, writing from his monastery in Jarrow around the year 730, is of a period of confusion and general disorder after the Romans left. The Britons, unused to having to defend themselves, called in mercenary bands from across the North

Sea to repel raiders from Ireland and Scotland. These fighters, coming from areas where there was pressure for more land, saw the potential of the country as a new home: warriors were followed by settlers.

Research into the etymology of place-names provides some clues about the origin of settlements. Names ending in '-*ham*' and '-*ton*', for example, denote an Anglo-Saxon homestead or farm, prefaced either by the name of the leader, or by some geographical or other distinguishing feature of the place. Names ending in '-*by*' or '-*thorpe*' are found in areas of later Scandinavian settlement.

The incomers were organised on a tribal basis, giving fierce loyalty to their chief who provided protection in return for service.

By the eighth century, the original tribal groups had coalesced into five Kingdoms of which Northumbria, covering the area north of the Humber, enjoyed a period of cultural pre-eminence until the Viking raids which started with the attack on Lindisfarne in 793. These targeted monasteries, centres of culture and learning where there was likely to be valuable treasure. By the eleventh century, one English kingdom had emerged, though constantly under threat from across the North Sea. The last Scandinavian invader was defeated at the battle of Stamford Bridge on the eve of the battle of Hastings. The country was divided into shires, under the administration of Earls appointed by the king from the families of the great magnates. In the shires that came under Scandinavian influence, the administrative sub-divisions known elsewhere as hundreds were called wapentakes, a word derived from 'the symbolic flourishing of weapons by which a public assembly confirmed its decisions',[1] a word which conjures up a picture of uneasy, dangerous times when no man went around unarmed.

The new settlers brought their own gods. Christianity, which had been a recognised religion within the Roman Empire since 312 and had a firm place in urban Romano-British society by the end of the Roman occupation, seems to have been driven westward to the 'Celtic fringes' of mainland Britain and to Ireland. It was brought back to northern England by missionary monks from Ireland by way of Iona,

---

[1] Stenton 497

and after 597 by the supporters of the mission dispatched from Rome under Augustine of Canterbury. These two traditions hammered out their differences at the Synod of Whitby in the year 664, with the advocates of the Celtic tradition giving way to the leaders of the Roman party.

The establishment of Christianity provided a cohesive element in the emergent English nation. The initial stage of the process of propagating the faith in Northumbria is related by Bede. He describes the austere and frugal life of the monastic communities at Lindisfarne and Streanaeshalch (Whitby), the zeal with which the priests from these communities went out sometimes for weeks at a time on preaching missions to the surrounding areas. According to Bede:

> *'If by chance a priest came to a village, the villagers crowded together, eager to hear from him the word of life; for the priests and the clerics visited the villages for no other reason than to preach, to baptise, and to visit the sick, in brief to care for their souls.'*[2]
>
> *'It was the custom among the English people at that time, when a clerk or priest came to a village, for all to gather at his command to hear the Word…'*[3]

Cuthbert, the greatly revered prior of Lindisfarne, *'used especially to make for those places and preach in those villages that were far away on steep and rugged mountains…'*.

At first, there was no parish structure in existence, no question of building a church or appointing a priest. Pastoral oversight was carried out by a group of clergy living according to a monastic rule in a monastery or minster. Three types of church came to be recognised by Anglo-Saxon law: the minsters, from which several priests covered a wide rural area; proprietory churches built by a lord for his estate, and field churches where a priest was permitted to say mass at an altar in the open field, the place perhaps marked by the erection of a stone cross. The evolution of a parochial system was a gradual process, still incomplete by the time of the Conquest.[4]

---

[2] Bede III 26
[3] Ibid IV 27
[4] Chibnall 195

Levisham

The scanty evidence of which to base any account of Levisham during the six centuries between the end of Roman occupation and the Norman Conquest lies in the name 'Levisham', and in various pieces of masonry discovered at or near the site of the church in the valley. This account suggests a course of events that fits the general picture of the period, and does not conflict with any of the existing evidence.

The name which was at different times written as 'Leuecen' (Domesday Book), 'Leuezham', (thirteenth century), 'Leasham' (seventeenth century) is likely to have been formed from the personal name of the leader of the group who made their home here – 'the homestead or village of a man called Leofgeat'.[5] It is believed that places with *–ham* suffixes are of an earlier date than place ending in *–ton*. Perhaps, then, we can imagine at some point during the early period of settlement Leofgeat and his clan in search of land to settle, moving up the valley from Pickering (originally *Pickeringham,* home of Pica's people). In turbulent, each-man-for-himself times, there would be attraction in a site with such clearly defined, defensible boundaries, where earlier farmers had cleared some of the forest, where there was good arable land on a gentle south-facing slope, springs in the valley sides, and iron to be found on the moor. Unlike their British predecessors who, in a more peaceful era, appear to have spread themselves over a wide area of the moor in dispersed homesteads, clearing fields and moving on when the soil was exhausted, the incomers preferred a nucleated settlement surrounded by their farm land. A system of cultivating the arable land communally in open fields, using a rotation that left each field fallow one year in three, was traditional for the Anglo-Saxons. The pattern of three open fields which formed the basis of Levisham farming until the end of the eighteenth century, may have been laid down at this period.

In Scarborough Museum there are miscellaneous bits of pottery, stone and metal from Bronze and iron Age settlements on Levisham moor, but nothing from this period – not surprising if the Anglo-Saxon village is deeply buried under the present village.

---

[5] Mills

Excavations on the site of the old church in the valley have produced some pieces of carved masonry from the Anglo-Saxon period: pieces of a cross shaft and a cross head which were incorporated in the walls of a later building,[6] and a stone grave-slab carved with the flowing lines of a mythical beast, which is now in the porch of the parish church. The archaeologists who worked on the site in 1977 recognised these stones as belonging to a Ryedale school of sculpture, similar to others sculpture found at Sinnington and Middleton, dating from the tenth century. They were surprised to find no trace at all of a church building from that period, not even post-holes from a wooden building. They found twelfth century remains at a lower level than the supposedly Saxon round headed, narrow chancel arch, and took this as evidence that the arch, though Saxon in architectural style, was the work of builders of Norman times who were not up-to-date with modern practices. They came to the conclusion that:

'though the Anglo-Scandinavian sculpture demonstrates that a tenth-century burial ground very probably existed on the site, there is no architectural evidence for any pre-Conquest fabric in the present church…'[7]

Was this perhaps the site of a field church, an outlying mission-post, marked by a stone cross? Or was the grave-slab, large and impressive enough to suggest a personage of some importance, that of a lord who had established a church of which no traces have yet been found? There is no mention of a church in either Levisham or Lockton in Domesday Book, but with only fifty places in the North Riding named as having churches it is thought they may have been under-recorded.[8]

The valley site, close to a ford across Levisham beck and near to the track (now a cart track) which was once the main road between Whitby and Pickering, would have been a likely spot for the kind of preaching place described by Bede. One could imagine the priests

---

[5] Mills

[6] in Ryedale Folk Museum, Hutton-le-Hole

[7] Yorkshire Archaeological Journal Vol.58 1986

[8] Darby & Maxwell 152-3

from Whitby or Lastingham tramping across the moors, finding this level spot near the ford a good place for setting up a cross, a place accessible to the villagers of Levisham on one side of the valley and Lockton on the other.

Following the Viking raids in the eighth century, the work and influence of monasteries and minsters declined. The establishment of a more permanent church awaited more settled times.

With no evidence for a church building or a priest in the village until the twelfth century, the question mark about a pre-conquest church must remain, part of the general obscurity of the period.

Credo. Melvyn Bragg *A novel, set in Northumbria in the time of the Abbess Hilda, giving*
Sceptre 1997 *an imaginative insight into an age about which so little is known with certainty.*

Chapter 4:
Under New Management
How things were organised after the Conquest

The chancel arch of St Mary's Church, believed to date from the twelfth century, is all that survives of the medieval building.

CHRONOLOGY

Date	National	Regional
1066: Sept.	Battle of Stamford Bridge	
1066: Oct.	Battle of Hastings	
1068-9		Rebellions by northern Earls Edwin and Morcar
1069		'Harrying of the North'
1085	Domesday Book	
1088		Rebellion involving some Yorkshire magnates
by 1106		Pickering Castle built
12th C		Intermittent fighting against Scots
1138		Battle of the Standard: Scots beaten near Northallerton
1348	Black Death	

SOURCES FOR LEVISHAM

On the ground	Documentary
Site of St Mary's Church; Chancel arch, font, grave slab with incised sword	Domesday Book
Lay-out of village	Levisham references in various published collections of medieval documents e.g. North Ridings Record Series

With more written sources available, the possibilities of reconstructing a picture of life at this period move on to surer ground. Domesday Book, compiled in 1085, provides information about the state of the country as it had been under Edward the Confessor and how it was two decades into the reign of William I. It is, however, not the comprehensive, infallible survey of the nation that is sometimes imagined, and there can be problems about its interpretation.

The nature of the records from this period restricts the picture they give. Literacy was confined to a small class of church-trained clerks, and records relate to transactions that had importance to the power structures of church and state. The King needed to keep track of what was owed to him in money or service, so there are records concerning the land-holdings of his tenants. Accounts were kept of taxes levied; records of court sessions and fines paid. The Church kept records of appointments to livings; monastic cartularies (collections of charters) contain documents relating to their lands and business transactions. From the point of view of the local historian this can give a skewed perspective. References to a village are likely to mention the lord of the manor, provide the name of the priest, refer to a monastic grange, but may throw little light on the life of the ordinary villagers. One problem for the average local historian is that Latin was the language of government and church, so that it is necessary to be able to read both the script and medieval Latin in order to be able to use original documents. However, there are a number of published translations of selected documents. The four volumes of the North Ridings Record Series contain annotated translations of a variety of documents relating to this area; others are to be found in the published volumes of the Yorkshire Archaeological Society. University libraries contain published volumes of calendars of Inquisitions and other State Papers.

The administrative unit during the medieval period was the manor, and some manorial records survive. These can be discovered from the Manorial Documents Register kept by the Historic Monuments Commission (accessible via the internet).

Background

1066 was a pivotal year in English history. The focus is usually on the battle of Hastings, but those living in the north east would have been more immediately aware of the battle of Stamford Bridge a month earlier.

The death in January of Edward the Confessor without an heir left a confused political situation full of potential danger. Harold Godwin's election to the throne did not have universal support. In May, his disaffected brother Tostig, outlawed after his removal from the Earldom of Northumbria, led a series of raids on the English coast.

Morcar, the new earl of Northumbria, mustered his forces to prevent Tostig landing in Yorkshire. Tostig then joined forces with the Norwegian king, Harald Hardrada, to invade England with a fleet sailing in September up the Humber, and on into the Ouse as far as Riccall. Leaving the fleet under guard, Harald and Tostig led a force of 6,000 men on the nine-mile march to York. Morcar and his brother Edwin, Earl of Mercia, met the invaders with a force of a similar size at Fulford. There was fierce fighting. Morcar and Edwin's men were driven back into marshy ground where they were slaughtered as they floundered in the mud. The way to York was open for Harald and Tostig, who received the surrender of the city on September 24th. Meanwhile, Harold with the English army had hastily marched north, perhaps not entirely confident of the loyalty of the northern Earls. His army surprised the Norwegians at Stamford Bridge as they made their way back to their ships at Riccall, defeating the last of the Norse invaders of England. Harald and Tostig were both killed in the battle. A week later, another invasion fleet set out to cross the Channel from Normandy. Harold's army set out on a forced march back south, but without the contingent of northern men they would have expected to join them. For Morcar's men, – no doubt including a contingent from his manor of Pickering, – the fighting in the year 1066 was in Yorkshire, not Sussex: they had suffered too great losses at the battle of Fulford to be in any condition to respond to the king's summons.

The conquest initiated a new era in English history. With land the source of wealth and power, the Conqueror used the transfer of land from the old English nobility to his own men as his method of control. Under the feudal system already in place land was held from the king in return for service of various kinds, the land-holders being in charge of the administration of law and order in the manors under their jurisdiction. The new regime brought in Normans, men of proven loyalty to the conqueror, to replace the former English manorial lords.

The Manor, the unit of local administration, operated through its Court Leet presided over by the Lord of the Manor assisted by his officials, the Steward or Seneschal and Bailiff, and also the representatives of the community, the Affeerors (=assessors) and panel of twelve Jurors. The court controlled the web of rights and responsibilities that held together the fabric of early medieval communities, dealing with issues of law and order, supervising the payment of dues, checking on boundaries by regular perambulations, overseeing the cultivation of the common fields. Gradually, over the centuries, the scope of the manorial courts was reduced; a few of these courts still survive, their role limited to management of the commons.[1]

The immediate aftermath of the Conquest in northern England was a series of revolts against the new regime which were crushed with such devastating severity that the economic life of the whole region was disrupted. Twenty years later, at the time of Domesday, the north was the most thinly populated area of the whole country with an estimated average of only 4 -5 inhabitants per square mile.[2] This was partly due to the greater amount of upland countryside, but also to the effects of the 'harrying of the north' by the Norman army in the winter of 1068-70 and to regular Scottish raids. This low point in the late eleventh century was followed by a century of recovery, when population in the north grew more rapidly than elsewhere. In 1377 the population of northern England has been estimated to have been seven times higher than in 1086, in spite of the Black Death which in the year 1348 caused the death of between a third and a half of the total population, bringing to an end a period of economic expansion during which more land was brought into cultivation than for centuries to come.

Castles made visible statements about power. Throughout the country people watched their new masters select strategic points to entrench themselves behind strong walls. From Scarborough to Helmsley ran a string of fortifications of which Pickering Castle was one, each a centre for

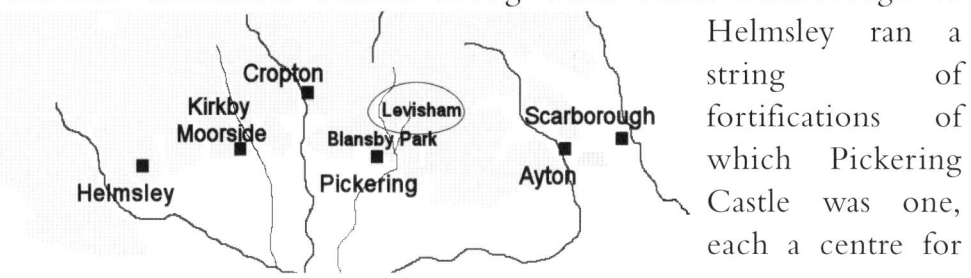

---

[1] In North Yorkshire: Danby, Spaunton, Fyling

[2] Miller & Hatcher

administration of the surrounding area.

During this period, church and crown worked in close collaboration. In medieval thinking, Church and State jointly represented the authority of God on earth, maintaining between them the divinely ordained order of the universe. The King encouraged monastic communities from Europe to establish houses in this country as agents of social and economic development, especially in Yorkshire, still relatively undeveloped compared with southern England.

The north of England was frontier territory, for three hundred years subject to repeated attacks from Scotland. The army of King David of Scotland got as far south as Northallerton in 1138 where they were beaten at the Battle of the Standard by an English army led by the Archbishop of York. Regular raids into the North Riding in the early fourteenth century were a sufficient menace for some communities to raise money to buy off the raiders. In 1322, Pickering offered 300 marks to Robert the Bruce, (a Scottish leader with local links, related to the de Brus family of Danby) to buy immunity from attack for the area between the River Seven to the coast. The hostages given as guarantees were still in Scotland three years later.[3]

There were always separatist tendencies in the north, the leading nobles looking back to the time when Northumbria had been an independent kingdom. The Earl of Northumbria was a figure the King of England could not afford to ignore.

Levisham

In 1066, Levisham along with a string of other villages in the area was attached to the manor of Pickering under the lordship of Morcar, Earl of Northumbria, one of the great magnates in the north of England. A member of one of the most powerful families in the whole kingdom, he was a key figure both in the events of 1066 and their aftermath.

While it may have mattered little to the men who ploughed the land who wore the English crown, the English nobility saw their power threatened by the Normans. Morcar was implicated in the

---

[3] NRR I. 4

series of rebellions in the north which provoked William I's retaliation, the so-called 'harrying of the north'. There is no way of knowing how this affected particular villages. Whether or not William's force went on the rampage through Levisham on their destructive campaign during the winter of 1069-70, we can be sure that the village shared in the disruption of normal agriculture and trade. It shows up in Domesday Book. After listing the villages linked with Pickering once held by Morcar, (thirteen, including Levisham) now held by the king, the report states: *'In all there are 50 carucates taxable which 27 ploughs can plough. Now there are only 10 villagers who have 2 ploughs. The rest is waste.'* The value of the manor of Pickering had been £88 in 1066; now it was assessed at 20s 4d. To envisage a work-force reduced from twenty seven plough-teams to two, an estate with its rateable value reduced to one eighth of its former worth, gives a measure of the calamity that had befallen the area. The next century saw recovery, overseen by the new management class put in place by the conquerors. Estimates based on the Poll Tax of 1377, a generation after the Black Death, put the population of Levisham at 56, in sixteen households – not so different from today.[4]

The Manorial System

By the twelfth century, the lordship of the manor of Levisham was held by the de Bolebec family – a name showing its Norman origins (Bolebec is a village in Normandy). Hugh de Bolebec figures in Domesday Book, holding several manors in Buckinghamshire. By the mid-twelfth century, there were Bolebecs holding land in Bedfordshire, Northumberland, Lincolnshire and Yorkshire.

A manor was an administrative unit, an area of jurisdiction, which could be a village, or a part of a village, or might include more than one village. While Levisham was one manor, there were four manors in Lockton, one of them held by the Levisham lord – a charter refers to Ralph de Bolebec's toft *'in the north part of Lockton near the lane which leads to Levisham'*, where there was sufficient pasture for 200 sheep.

[4] Allerston

In an attempt to prevent any one man from becoming too powerful, William I's policy was for one man's land-holdings to be in different parts of the country, for example Ralph de Bolebec who held the manor of Levisham also had the larger manor of Fulstow in Lincolnshire. On his journeys between Fulstow and Levisham he would no doubt be glad to avail himself of the hospitality offered to him by William, Prior of Malton: *'we have granted to our beloved Ralph de Bolebec perpetual and honourable sustenance with two horses and two men to minister to him as often as he comes to us…'*.[5]

Between the twelfth and mid-thirteenth centuries there was a succession of at least three generations of Levisham manorial lords with the name Ralph de Bolebec. A charter issued around 1220 by the second Ralph refers to *'my demesne and that of my ancestors'*[6] which suggests that the line went back still further. The last Bolebec connected with Levisham was Osbert, brother of Ralph who had died without heirs in 1252. Osbert sold his title to one of the Bigod family: a manor by this time had become a piece of property that could be bought and sold, subject to royal approval. During the following centuries, the manor of Levisham passed to a number of different owners, none of them known to have any personal link with the place. The new owners should be thought of, perhaps, as company directors, for whom one small piece of property in North Yorkshire was a minor item on their balance sheet.

Bolebec Lords of the Manor: 1160 (or earlier) - 1255

Approx. dates	Name	What we know	Source
1160 – 1200	Ralph I	references to office of Forester[7]	Pipe Rolls
1203 – 1220	Ralph II	Grant to Malton Priory	NRR IV p188-192
1230's – 1252	Ralph III	dealings with Malton Priory	Malton Cartulary
1253 – 55	Osbert	sold land and office of forester to Bigod	II p 226 NRR

---

[5] Malton Cartulary

[6] NRR IV. 188

[7] see chapter on Forest and Forest Law

The 12th and 13th centuries, the period when the village was under Bolebec management was one of significant development from the depopulated vill that has its brief mention in Domesday Book to a viable community of an estimated sixteen families in 1377.

Levisham shares with a number of other villages in this region a layout which has all the appearance of planning: a wide main street flanked by regular-sized plots backing onto a back lane. This is not the way a village develops naturally; in Lastingham, for example, you can see an unplanned village, with houses and lanes straggling in haphazard way from a central nucleus. The suggestion has been made that the layout of these apparently planned villages, (which were all pre-existing settlements) dates from the twelfth century, and was part of a deliberate recovery plan.[8] Perhaps we can envisage Ralph de Bolebec, anxious to turn his Levisham holding into a viable economic unit, discussing with some of his fellow manorial lords the best lay-out for a village, the optimum size for a house plot, before setting about the task of reconstructing the village.

The layout of Levisham: possibly a planned 12th century village

The lanes that we know today leading out of Levisham northwards onto the moor appear to have been in place by the mid-thirteenth century, when in a deed granting land to the Canons of Malton Priory, there is reference to '...*land ...between the roads leading to the moor...in the place called Dundale.*' The deed concerns:

> '...*52 acres of land in Levisham of which 23 acres lay between his own flat of arable land and the dyke towards the north and*

---

[8] Allerston

between the road leading to the moor, in the place called Dundale, and 29 acres to the west of the western road.'[9]

Using the details given in this deed, it is possible to surmise that Bolebec's desmene land (*'his own flat of arable land'*) was probably the land between the lanes – land which was never part of the three open fields. The 23 acres *'…between his own flat of arable land and the dyke towards the north…'* would match the fields numbered 232 – 238 on the Tithe Map, the 29 acres to the west of the western road plots 224 – 230, another area not part of the open fields, described as 'old enclosure' at the time of the 1770 Enclosure.

The provision of a church would have been part of this enterprise, its site between Lockton and Levisham partly determined by the pre-existing burial-ground and possible earlier church, partly to serve the Bolebec's Lockton tenants as well as the people of Levisham. A twelfth century date for the church fits both the archaeological findings and the absence of mention of a church in Domesday Book. Preserved within the chancel of the now ruined

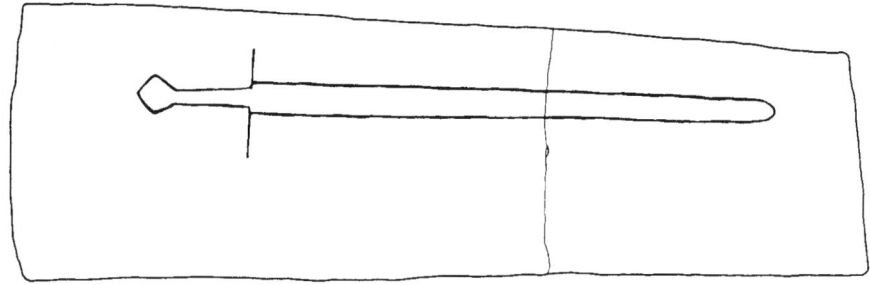

12th century grave stone carved with incised sword from Levisham Church

church is a stone grave-slab incised with a cross, dated by the archaeologists as most likely from the mid-twelfth or possibly the thirteenth century. Was it a memorial to one of the Bolebecs? The third Ralph arranged for his body to be buried at Malton Priory, so the grave is not his.[10] It could be that of the first Ralph, fitting the preference of the archaeologists for a twelfth century date, and fitting also the supposition that he was the builder of the church, someone likely to be honoured with a special tomb.[11]

[9] Malton Cartulary

[10] Malton Cart.

[11] Hall & Lang

There is nothing to suggest that any of the medieval manorial lords lived in Levisham on a permanent basis. However, in the field above the church is a level area identified by archaeologists as a house-platform. The site has never been excavated, but fragments of medieval pottery can be picked up there, turned up in the molehills. One theory is that this was the parsonage; another that it was the manor house where the Bolebecs and their successors lodged when in Levisham.

The manor was administered through the Court Leet, presided over by the manorial lord or his representative. There are records of the proceedings of the Levisham Court Leet in the nineteenth century when its real power had long gone, but its structure and some of its terminology recall the time when it was the controlling agency of the

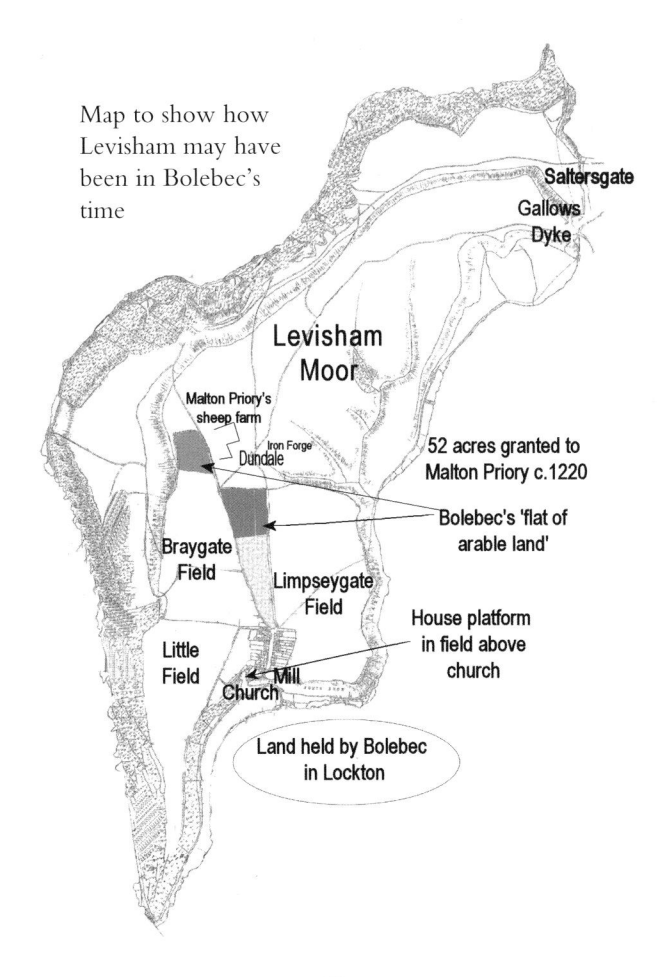

Map to show how Levisham may have been in Bolebec's time

village. This nineteenth century Court Book still used the phrase 'View of Frankpledge', which dates back to Anglo-Saxon customs by which groups of households held corporate responsibility for the actions of their members for which they were answerable to a twelve-man jury sworn in at the Court Leet.[12] In 1891, the Court Leet records report the Perambulation of the Parish boundaries carried out by eleven court members. Starting at the Mill, they followed Levisham Beck northwards to the Hole of Horcum, there

> *'turning northwest to the top of the hill by Gallow Dyke and then turning northeast down the Hill …the boundary at this point being marked by several boundary stones and then in a Northerly direction into a deep gully locally called Trowlsarse and then following the downward course of the Beck until it joins Pickering Beck in Newton Dale…'*[13]

– following in the footsteps of generations of their forebears. Where in more recent days the court was imposing small fines for encroachments on common rights, in medieval times this was the court through which law and order in all its aspects was maintained. A document from the thirteenth century confirmed that Roger Bigod had the gallows at Levisham (presumably sited at Gallows Dyke) and the Assize of Bread and Ale,[13] a tax on basic commodities levied by the lord. Behind the brief documentary references couched in unfamiliar language we can glimpse an ordered, structured village society. We hear of Adam the reeve, the bailiff or steward of the manor,[14] holding a bovate of land down by the church, Hugh of Lockton who conducted business on Bolebec's behalf,[15] William the chamberlain,[16] Robert le Bel the rector,[17] – all men with responsible positions in manorial administration.

Iron was produced in Levisham throughout the medieval period. From the Bolebecs onwards, there are records of payments of two shillings a year to the Exchequer for an iron forge on Levisham Moor. The iron at Levisham and the salt produced at their manor of

---

[12] Levisham Court Book
[13] Levisham Court Book
[14] English
[15] Malton Cart.fol 117v
[16] Malton Cart. fol.118r
[17] Assize Roll. 139

Fulstow would have been important economic assets to the Bolebecs, together with the revenue from Levisham mill (first mentioned in thirteenth century documents) and the agricultural produce from the demesne land, the lord's home farm, cultivated on his behalf by his tenants.

Bolebec III had a long absence when he went on a Crusade, selling some of his Fulstow land to Malton Priory to cover his expenses.[18] On his return in 1246 he was embroiled in a law-suit in York. A document bearing Bolebec's seal was produced by the plaintiff, Thomas Hoggshagh, apparently an agreement made before Ralph set out for the Holy Land when he was setting his affairs in order in case he did not return. Ralph disputed the authenticity of the document, saying that his seal had been left with the Prior of Malton for safe keeping during his absence. *'If anyone put his seal to the said writing, it was sealed after he had set out to the Holy Land and after he had handed over his seal to the Prior to keep.'* As the case was settled by Ralph agreeing to grant *'to Thomas and his heirs a rent of half a mark, to be taken yearly... from Ralph's mill at Levesham...'*, it looks as if his defence did not stand up in court.[19]

The Inquisition Post Mortem held after the death of the last Ralph de Bolebec's death in 1252 takes us into the world of feudalism at the grass root level. Such an inquest was required after the death of any tenant-in-chief of the king to establish the details of his tenure, and to determine who was his heir: who would pay the bills in future. On April 22nd 1252 twelve men from the area, the list headed by Ralph of Lockton and John the younger of Newton, formed the jury that gathered in Levisham. They confirmed that Ralph held twenty-six bovates (around three hundred acres) of land in Levisham, some directly from the king but most from the Earl of Albermarle – an important figure in the region of Holderness. There is reference to 'free men' who were sub-tenants of Ralph, paying rent for a further six bovates. The mill is valued, also the church – at this date a piece of real estate belonging to its patron. The inquisition concludes by confirming that Ralph's brother, Osbert was the next heir, *'but where*

[18] Inqu.P.M.   [19] Owen p.125

he is the jurors know not'.[20] Wherever he was, Osbert had no interest in his brother's Yorkshire properties which he soon disposed of.

Summary

By assembling the various references to Levisham in documents from the eleventh to the thirteenth centuries, it is possible to construct a picture that fits with the evidence on the ground. According to this picture, at the time of the Conquest, Levisham was one of several very small settlements (vills) within the Manor of Pickering. Following the dislocation of normal life during the generation following the Conquest, Levisham was assigned as a manor to a member of the de Bolebec family. During the second half of the twelfth century, under the management of the first Ralph de Bolebec who can be clearly identified, Levisham was rebuilt in a planned manner, following the contemporary trend in the area, with a street running on a north-south axis bordered by regular sized plots for a house with a garth behind.

To serve his tenants in Levisham and Lockton, Bolebec built a church in the valley on the site of an existing burial-ground, incorporating pieces of earlier carved stone crosses into its masonry, and appointed a priest. He was buried in this church, his grave marked by a stone slab decorated with a sword.

The economic life of the village was enhanced by the provision of a mill in the valley beside the beck, and by the exploitation of iron in the Dundale area on the moor, using the abundant wood from the area to make charcoal for smelting. Prosperity was further increased by the establishment of a Monastic Grange managed by Malton Priory to the north of the village.

By the middle of the 13th century when Osbert de Bolebec sold the Manor to Bigod, Levisham was established as a small but viable agricultural community.

---

[20] YAS vol. LXVII p139

[21] Calendar of Inquisitions vol.I Henry III p.32-2

> **Manor of Levisham**
>
> To Wit The Court-Leet, View of Frank Pledge and Court-Baron of James Walker Esquire Lord of the said Manor of Levisham in the County of York held at Levisham aforesaid in and for the said Manor on Friday the fifteenth day of October one thousand eight hundred and fifty eight Before William North Gentleman Steward of the said Court: —
>
> ### The names of the Jury
>
> John Wilson, Foreman, Sworn
>
> | | | |
> |---|---|---|
> | George Chester — Sw | John Toad — Sw | |
> | John Coulson — Sw | William Jackson — Sw | William Thompson — Sw |
> | William Craven — Sw | Robert Head — Sw | John Vasey — Sw |
> | William Dixon — Sw | William Sedman — Sw | Hassall Newton — Sw |
> | John Estill — Sw | Joseph Head — Sw | |
>
> John Toad, Constable — Sworn
>
> Daniel Collins, Pindar, Sworn
>
> John Pennock } Afferors, Sworn.
> Matthew Dixon }
>
> We the Jurors sworn at this Court do upon our Oaths present and amerce the several persons hereinafter named at the several sums set opposite to their respective names for cutting and digging Turves upon the Commons and Wastes within this Manor, they having respectively no right so to do, namely
>
> Robert Hansell in respect of his House in Newton Dale, which has not a Common right, in the sum of two pence

A page from the Levisham Court Book, in the year 1852 still using the forms and terminology of the medieval court

Chapter 5:
Forest and Forest Law

Pickering Castle: one of the string of strongholds between Scarborough and Helmsley from which royal power was exercised, and the Royal Forest administered.

CHRONOLOGY

1106	Pickering Forest established
1215	Forest Law modified in Magna Carta
1217	Forest Charter
1639	Pickering disafforested

SOURCES

On the ground	Documentary
Pickering Castle	Various documents relating to enforcement of Forest Law included in North Riding Records Series
Blansby Park	

The four volumes of the North Ridings Record Society series contain documents relating to the Honour and Forest of Pickering translated and edited by the Victorian antiquarian, Robert Turton. Most of the references in this section have been taken from this invaluable quarry of information.

Background

Royal Forests predated the Conquest, but under the Norman kings their area was expanded, especially in the less populated and less intensively farmed parts of England. The Norman influence can be seen in the words with a French derivation in the forest system, terms such as 'vert' for vegetation, 'verderers' and 'regarders', the officials on the lookout for offences.

The largest of the forests was Pickering Forest, founded in 1106, stretching from the river Seven, the tributary to the Rye which flows down through Rosedale, to the coast, a forest area so extensive that it was divided into two wards, the west ward running from the Seven to East Ayton, the east ward sometimes called Scalby Forest.

Like a National Park today, a designated 'Forest' included within its boundaries towns, villages, arable land, moorland as well as actual woodland. The essential feature of a Forest was administrative: in addition to the common law of the land it was subject to the

The Royal Forest of Pickering

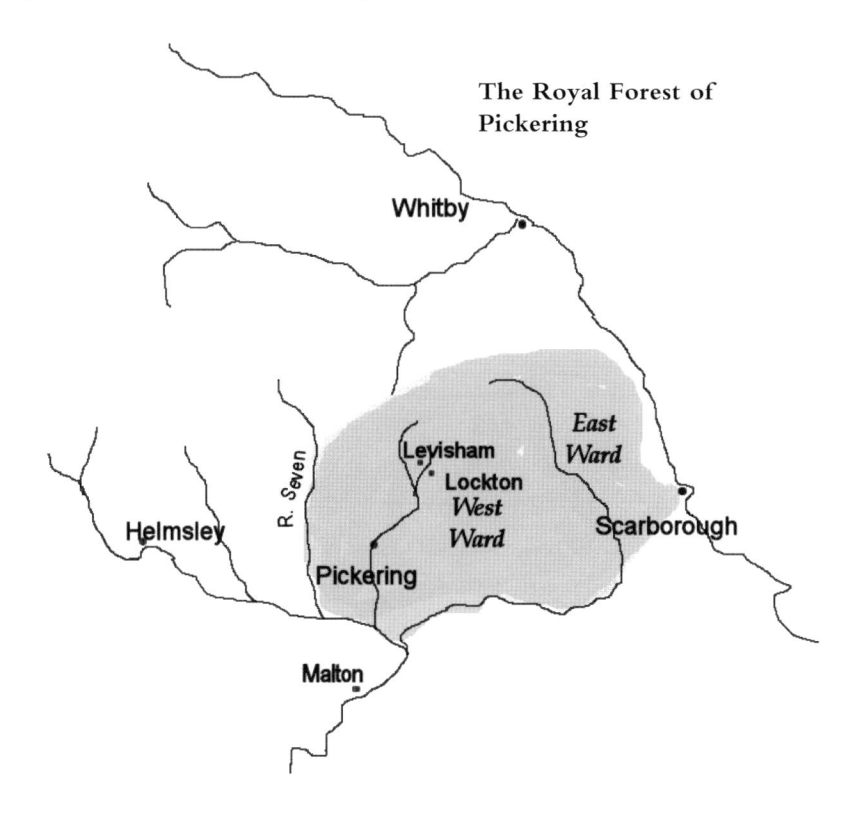

provisions of Forest Law. Inhabitants of Forest areas lived surrounded by resources that they were prohibited from using – timber for building, wood for fuel, (except what could be reached 'by hook or by crook'), game for food; these economic assets were reserved to the Crown. Dogs kept within the forest were required to be 'lawed', that is, have three claws from the front foot removed (to impede their hunting ability) – a provision that in time came to be changed to a money payment, 'hungeld', a form of dog-license. The carrying of bows and arrows was banned: regulation after regulation, making Forest Law deeply unpopular. Some grievances were addressed in Magna Carta and in the Forest Charter two years later, but the law continued to be so unpopular as to be virtually unenforceable. Its operation declined along with the power of the monarchy in the late fourteenth and the fifteenth centuries. Tudor and Stuart monarchs attempted to revive it, seeing the forests as a source of natural resources such as timber for ship building and as a means of raising revenue, but without success and Forest Law was abolished in 1660.

Forest Officials

The administration of such an extensive enterprise required a complex hierarchy of officials.

At the top was the Warden or Steward, a royal appointee usually also in charge of a castle. His was a lucrative post, often hereditary. Next came the Foresters-in-Fee, two for each ward of Pickering Forest. They too were royal officials whose hereditary position carried a range of rights and privileges. The Levisham Bolebecs held one of these posts and passed it on to the Bigods, the office linked with land that they held. Under them came various ranks of foresters – the men who actually did the work of patrolling and checking. In 1322, the accounts of Pickering Castle list the wages of a forester at 2d a day.[1] At the bottom of the ladder were the woodwards, an axe their insignia of office.

The County Courts appointed their own officers, Verderers, Regarders and Agisters to keep a check on the way the law was being kept – a thankless job, so unpopular that some were prepared to pay for exemption. They were responsible to the Local Attachment Courts, held every forty days to deal with minor offences.

Periodically Royal Justices travelled round the country holding a Forest Eyre at which a panel of twelve Regarders presented the results of their survey of the state of the forest. They were required to report on any land that had been enclosed and cultivated or built on ('assarted'); they were to count and write down every stump of oak or beech, to note where hawks and falcons nested and check on who was entitled to them. From honey to mineral rights, everything going on in the forest was, in theory, to be checked up on and reported to the court.[2] It is not surprising to learn that in 1334, *'several men forcibly impeded the regarders from making their regard in Raincliff...'*.[3] All these administrative details counted for nothing when the machinery failed to operate. When the Justices arrived at Pickering Castle to hold a Forest Eyre in 1334, it was the first to be held for over thirty years: gradually, the whole system fell into disuse.

[1] NRR IV. 207
[2] NRR II. 238-241
[3] NRR III.16

From 1168 onwards there are regular references to Ralph de Bolebec holding the office of Forester of Scarborough Forest, the East Ward of the extensive Forest of Pickering. An enquiry in 1320 established that *'from time immemorial Ralph de Bolebec and his ancestors were stewards of the Forest and Foresters in Fee…'*.[4]

Levisham

The first time we are introduced to Levisham inhabitants by name and learn something about their occupations and their activities is in the court records relating to the Forest. There are long lists of offenders, naming the offence and the court verdict. In May 1293 we meet Ralph the miller, outlawed for taking a hind on the mill cliff below Levisham;[5] his son William followed in his father's footsteps, and was caught hunting a hind to death on the moor between Pickering and Kingthorpe, and outlawed. A few years later, William was again before the court and outlawed along with Richard Wroth, the woodward of Levisham, for killing a hind. Outlawry was clearly not a deterrent to lawbreaking: to be put outside the protection of the law would not be a problem for those who were confident of support within their community. William Settrington, another Levisham woodward, was accused of killing a hart with bow and arrow in Newtondale, and it was further alleged that *'he was wont to place sharp spears in hedges to catch deer'*.[6] In the recorded lists of names of offenders brought before the justices in Pickering, are John of Levisham, Walter of Levisham, Geoffrey Wylen of Levisham….so it goes on.

Sometimes there are longer reports of incidents that read like the sort of thing we find in the local press today:

'On Thursday, 29 July, 1305, two hinds, which had been taken or hunted, were found by Nicholas, son of William Lockton, in two trenches cut under ground at Trollesers, near Saltergate. The trenches had been dug by John Morolf and Alexander Piper for the purpose of hiding game which had been stolen from the forest and

---

[4] NRR III. 242

[5] NRR II. 88

[6] NRR II. 92

salted, and when Nicholas came upon them and found what they were doing they would have slain him had not two men from Levisham come to his assistance …'.[7]

'John Shepherd, Parson of Levisham, said to be son of Ralph Story and John son of John Clerk of the same on Sunday 25th of August 1336 came into Houghdale with bows and arrows and killed a hart, and were caught in the act by Edmund Hastyngs, acting as forester for Parnell de Kynthorp, forester of fee. They were taken to Pickering Castle and delivered to Ralph Hastings then constable of the same…'.[8]

As well as poaching, there were 'offences of vert', when trees were felled for house-building, for making sheep folds, for firewood or making charcoal. We read of William, Rector of Levisham being fined 3s 4d for one green oak;[9] John de Melsa, Lord of the Manor of Levisham in the early fourteenth century, paying 6s 8d compensation for making charcoal in Levisham woods for his iron forge.[10]

Throughout the records of these court proceedings we are aware that offenders were as likely to be from those classes of society generally found of the side of law and order as from the so-called 'lower orders', reinforcing the sense of the universal detestation with which these forest laws were held. After a period when forest law lapsed into disuse, there was a spurt of activity when the Tudor monarchs attempted its revival. In 1488, John Consett, yeoman, (the bearer of a name common in Levisham until the eighteenth century), was found not guilty of the offence for which he was brought to court, but during Elizabeth's reign William Watson, the Rector of Levisham was unable to wriggle out of responsibility for his misdemeanour. Acting on information received, on January 23rd 1585 the law enforcers visited the house of William Watson, and reported to the court:

'…we made diligent search and enquiry….we did learn that we should find venison and crossbows……we riding to one William Watson, Clerk, Parson of Levisham, a town that stands in the

[7] NRR II. 83
[8] NRR II. 114
[9] NRR IV. 37
[10] NRR IV. 60

heart of the forest the 23rd Jan last past did there find in his house 1 crossbow of weight 4lb and certain venison baked in the said house and so examined further of the said venison and bow how and by what means it came thither; by much enquiry and diligence we got out the killing both of red & fallow deer....'

Watson had two accomplices, both keepers under Sir Richard Cholmley. He admitted hunting in Newtondale with one of these men and sharing with him the hind that they killed. He owned to having shot a male deer with a cross bow the previous year; about Michelmas he went out with his long bow and took a buck; between Christmas and the new year he and his dog got a fawn, and on January 15th he killed a fallow deer with his greyhound. Quite a sportsman!

By the reign of James I when the Surveyor General, James Norden, was sent to conduct a survey of the Royal Forests, it was the value to the national economy of the timber that predominated rather than game preservation, and the recorded fines are for felling of trees and for making enclosures or 'assarts' from forest land. In 1621, a Levisham carpenter, Thomas Payte, was fined 8 shillings for taking an oak from Newtondale and investigations were made into the ownership of assarts within the boundaries of Levisham.[11]

While the local inhabitants were carrying out their illegal activities, the legitimate hunting for which the Forests had been established was being carried on. The Forests supplied meat to the Royal larder. In 1229, the Sheriff of York was notified that venison from Pickering Forest would be delivered to him by the king's huntsmen, Guy, John and Philip, which was to be salted and kept.[12] King John and his court, while in residence at Nottingham in 1251, were able to feast on boar sent down from Pickering forest. King Henry III had two huntsmen, William and Richard Candover, who were sent from time to time to the Forest of Pickering to hunt for deer which were salted and dispatched to Westminster. There is a note to the Sheriff of York (1261):

[11] NRR I. 19 and 30   [12] Liberate Rolls 1226-40

'Let William and Richard Candover, King's huntsmen, whom he is sending to the Forest of Pickering with stag hounds to take stag there, have 10 marks...'.

The next year the Sheriff received instructions

'...to salt well 80 stags which William and Richard Candover the King's huntsmen will take in the Forest of Pickering and deliver to him, and to carry them to Westminster against the Feast of St. Edward for delivery to keepers of the larder by the 3rd or 4th day before the feast.' [13]

Pickering Castle accounts include expenses of foresters, bowmen, and hounds employed in taking 10 harts, the cost of 2 quarters 4 bushels of salt at 2s 6d a quarter, casks to put them in and the hire of a cart to take them to York.

Looking south across the steep valley of Newtondale from Ness Head, the southernmost tip of Levisham, lies Blansby Park, an enclosed deer park attached to Pickering Castle which during the fourteenth century housed a royal stud. Every year, grooms brought up stallions from London to serve the breeding mares kept at Blansby Park. Sometimes actual names are recorded – in 1326, two black stallions, Morell of Merton and Morell of Tutbury were delivered by Adam de Hodesden, King's Master of the Horse, who took back with him six horses from the last year's three-year-olds, for the King's use.

The accounts for the Blansby Park operation for the years 1322 and 1326 detail the expenses incurred in maintaining around twenty mares and their progeny: the repair of their houses, the cost of cart-loads of hay and oats, the purchase of canvas and woollen cloth for saddle-cloths, and of honey for greasing bridles. There were grooms and blacksmiths to be employed, men to do maintenance work on the buildings and fences. There was much coming and going. William de London, the King's carter, his groom and six horses were in residence in Pickering. When there was need to be in touch with their royal master, a messenger was sent – 3d a day for 9 days.

Throughout the medieval period Pickering Castle stood above the town, a powerful symbol of the royal authority that exercised such intrusive regulation of life in the area. Inhabitants of villages within

---

[13] Liberate Rolls vol. 5

the Forest of Pickering could not avoid having their lives circumscribed by the provisions of Forest Law. The chronicler who complained that the exactions of the Forest Court had '*reduced the whole country from coast to coast to beggary*'[14] was no doubt expressing a general mood. But the castle and all its ramifications as the administrative centre of the forest also acted as a focus for economic growth by providing jobs. Its impact on the economy of the surrounding villages must have been considerable. We can imagine the Levisham forge supplying iron for the horseshoes and nails listed in the accounts, and village men lining up to be hired at 1½d a day at hay-making time.

The history of one particular village cannot be investigated in isolation. Its life, its economy, is inevitably bound up with the life and economy of the surrounding region. Levisham, along with all the other villages of the region, might be a long way from the centres of power, but the life of the village, then as now, was significantly shaped by the institutions and policies of national government.

---

[14] Roger de Hovedene, quoted Grant.

Chapter 6:
Monks as Farmers

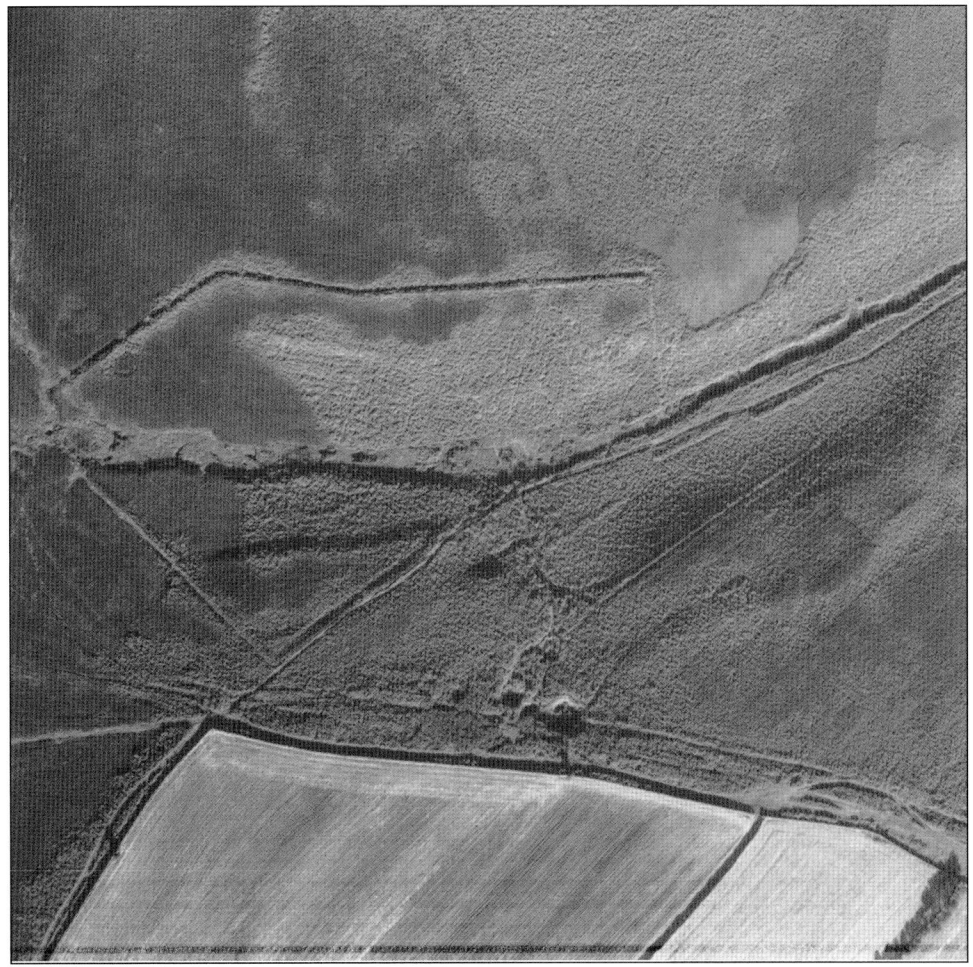

Medieval Sheep Farm in Dundale on Levisham Moor: the outline of its perimeter bank and ditch seen clearly in this aerial photograph. © Crown Copyright NMR

CHRONOLOGY

c.1078	Benedictine Monastery founded at Whitby
1130-60	Cistercian Monasteries at Rievaulx, Fountains, Byland. Gilbertine Priory at Malton. Women's Monastic Houses at Wykeham, Yeddingham, Rosedale, Keldholme, Baysdale
13th century	Monastic grange at Levisham

SOURCES

On the ground	Documentary
Monastic ruins	Malton Cartulary
Old Malton Parish Church	
Site of Monastic Grange on Levisham Moor	

To visit the remains of one of the great North Yorkshire monasteries gives a sense of their size and status, even when little is now left. The exhibitions provided at sites such as Rievaulx and Whitby illuminate the various aspects of medieval monastic life, the hidden life of prayer and study and the engagement in the practicalities of farming and business. The present Parish Church of Old Malton once formed part of the nave of the church of St Mary's Priory: it is just one third of the original church, yet even today is a large and impressive building. The Priory when it was first built, towering over the wattle-and-daub cottages of twelfth century Malton, was making a powerful statement about the wealth and importance of monastic establishments in medieval society.

Monastic houses kept their official business papers – documents concerning land, accounts, – in their *Cartulary* [collection of charters]. In the Malton Cartulary are documents relating to Ralph de Bolebec's grant of land in Levisham which is discussed below.

Background

The monastic ruins that are such an impressive feature of the North Yorkshire landscape date from the century after the Conquest, when monastic orders from the continent were encouraged to set up houses in England and enjoyed a period of remarkable expansion and popularity.

A change had come over the monastic world since the days of Hilda's abbey in Whitby. Religious houses were no longer outposts of a faith struggling to win over the rulers and population of a largely heathen land; they had become collaborators with the secular authorities in the ordering of a Christian nation, with the resources to put up buildings of a scale and magnificence previously unknown.

St. Benedict's Rule (dating from the sixth century) provided the basis for the monasticism that flourished in medieval Europe. It set out a way of life for celibate communities to live apart from but related to the world, engaged in prayer and study but also in practical work, supporting themselves by their labour and serving society by their charitable works. Various Orders were founded, each with its distinctive characteristics. There were Orders of monks living within the enclosure of their monasteries in remote places; Orders of canons, priests living in community under a Rule, working from Priories in centres of population. Friars such as the Franciscans and Dominicans were out and about preaching and working with the poor, Orders of knights, the Templars and Hospitallers crusading and protecting pilgrims. The Cistercians became one of the most influential Orders in England. Founded at Citeaux in 1098, they practised a reformed, stricter observance of the Benedictine Rule. They chose to establish themselves in remote places where their communities could engage in their simple, industrious style of life with manual work sharing importance with prayer and study.

Paradoxically, communities whose members were individually dedicated to a life of poverty and prayer became wealthy, powerful bodies, influential in the economic and political world. In an age when the majority of the population lived at subsistence level, these were communities recruited mainly from the upper levels of society, their members literate, with access to books and to the best medical knowledge. Their living accommodation was of a standard far above that of the average family, their diet simple but wholesome and balanced. They lived a disciplined, ordered life, and as single-sex communities were not burdened with the need to provide for a dependent family. Their international links helped them to become centres of what would today be known as 'best practice' in the enterprises that they undertook.

Following the 'harrying of the north', Yorkshire was ripe for re-settlement: religious orders were the agency for its development, invading the area in a 'monastic blitzkrieg'.[1] Barons granted land to religious communities recognising their capability to convert wasteland into productivity. When Walter Espec, the lord of Helmsley, gave the Augustinian Canons land at Kirkham in 1130 and welcomed the Cistercians into the Rye valley in 1132, he was making provision both for the development of his land – and, he hoped, for the eternal welfare of his soul.

Those living in the Levisham area in the early thirteenth century had a dozen or more religious communities in easy reach. Within a radius of twenty miles was the Benedictine abbey of Whitby to the north, with cells at Goathland and Hackness. To the west lay the prestigious Cistercian abbeys of Rievaulx and Byland. The Augustinians had their abbey at Kirkham, the Gilbertines a priory at Malton, while the Knights Templar had a preceptory at Foulbridge on the river Derwent which was later passed on to the Knights

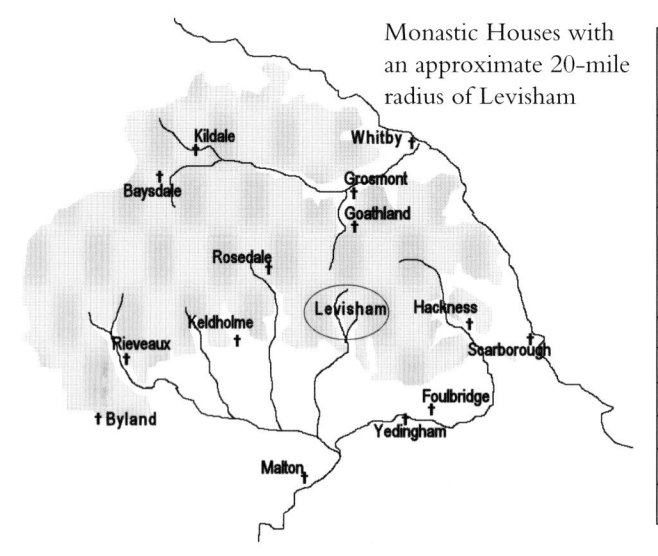

Monastic Houses with an approximate 20-mile radius of Levisham

Benedictine monks	Whitby; cells at Goathland and Hackness
Benedictine nuns	Yedingham
Cistercian monks	Rievaulx Byland
Cistercian nuns	Keldholme Rosedale Wykeham Baysdale
Augustine Canons	Kirkham
Gilbertine Canons	Malton
Dominican Friars	Scarborough
Crutched Friars	Kildale
Grandmontine canons	Grosmont
Knights Templar	Foulbridge

[1] Waites: Monasteries and the Landscape. p. 66

Hospitaller. There were smaller women's houses at Rosedale, Yedingham, Keldholme, Wykeham and Baysdale.

When Cistercians were offered land at a distance from their house, they organised it as a self-contained outlying farm or Grange run by lay brothers with additional hired labourers, all under the oversight of the monastery. Other orders, including the Priory at Malton, took up this practice.

The Gilbertine Canons of Malton belonged to the only English foundation amongst the religious orders, their Malton Priory becoming one of their wealthiest houses. It ran three hospitals for feeding the poor in Malton, and to finance its charitable work engaged in extensive sheep farming from which it derived two thirds of its income – about £400 in a good year, according to accounts from the first half of the thirteenth century.[2] Under an expansionist Prior, William of Ancaster (1244 – 67) Malton Priory was on the look out for potential donors of land. Their accounts during this period show that they had land in 49 parishes, all within a day's walking distance of the mother-house. During the second half of the thirteenth century the sheep farming of the monastic granges in north Yorkshire was big business. Sheep thrived on the moorlands, and the monasteries like multinational corporations today had the connections and the expertise to be able to exploit the international market for wool, handling bulk orders from Flemish and Italian merchants in a way that would have been impossible for small producers.[3]

Levisham

From the eighteen documents in the Malton Cartulary concerning Levisham we can get some insight into the process by which monasteries acquired land for a grange. Most of them relate to land granted to the priory by the lord of the Manor of Levisham, Ralph Bolebec. Some are dated, others can be dated approximately through references they contain. The first, dating from around 1220, concerns the grant of fifty-two acres of land *'in the territory of Levisham…in the place called Dundale'*. The location is described:

---

[2] V C. H. Vol. III. 253   [3] Waites.188-195

'*twenty-three acres…between my strip of arable land and the ditch facing north…*' and another twenty-nine acres further the west. The charter goes on to detail all that is included in the grant: '*…sufficient pasture for one thousand sheep and one hundred and twenty other animals…*'. The canons were to have wood to build their houses and fences, turf and heath to use as they wished. They could collect winter fodder and make sheep-folds in the woods.[4]

The location of what is presumed to be the site of this monastic grange can be discerned today beneath the heather and bracken on the moor, the outline of the boundary ditches and fences picked out on aerial photographs, the perimeter ditches to the west and north still clearly defined as you walk round them. You can see the levelled platform for some large building, and the stone foundations of other buildings. The likelihood is that there would have been farm buildings – granary, barns, animal house, and simple living accommodation for the few resident lay brothers with perhaps a small chapel.

The site straddles a small valley running down to Dundale Pond which was no doubt used for watering the stock. An area nearby shows traces of ridge-and-furrow field systems. While it is impossible to be certain where the various pieces of land referred to in the charters lie, by walking over the area with maps and the text of the Bolebec grants, it is possible at least to say 'perhaps here…?' and to guess the location of the arable plots.

This original grant was confirmed by Ralph's son and successor, (another Ralph), and again by his successor, Osbert. A charter of 1250 granted to the Priory Levisham mill and additional land in the valley to the south of the church. There are records of Inquisitions held on different occasions when a twelve-man jury checked on the legal status of the Prior of Malton's tenure of these Levisham lands.

Further light is thrown on these transactions by other charters in the cartulary. The opening paragraph of the first charter states: '*…for the sake of divine charity and for my salvation and the souls of my ancestors…*'. Here, it seems, in an age of faith, was a pious man investing some of his worldly goods to secure his future in the next world.

---

[4] Malton Cart. fol.116v

However, two charters of a rather different kind open up another angle on the transaction. These are charters or Starrs,[5] one issued by Leo, son of Solomon the Jew of Lincoln, the other by Aaron, son of Josce the Jew of York. An investigation of what lies behind these documents reveals a situation much more complex than the first charter quoted above would suggest.

Following the Conquest, Jews had been encouraged to settle in England where for two centuries they enjoyed royal protection, their financial backing facilitating the expansion of trade and agriculture, their taxes helping to pay for foreign wars. Officially, the Church frowned on the practice of lending out money at interest – 'usury' – but with no banking system in operation, Bishops and Heads of Monasteries as well as secular personages found it necessary to have recourse to the service the Jewish financiers provided. There were periodic outbreaks of anti-Jewish violence in Lincoln and York (their big financial centres), but they were assured of the King's support so long as their wealth flowed into the royal coffers in the form of heavy taxes. When by 1290 they had been taxed to the point where they were no longer useful, they were expelled from the country.

The Starr of Leo the Jew reads as follows:

'Know all men that the quitclaim to the Prior and convent of Malton of all things which Ralph de Bolebec named in pure and perpetual alms, namely in his land and pasture of Levisham, the pasture of 1,000 sheep and 120 animals with their families of three years and three stallions and similarly the site of a sheepfold and the site of animal houses, by name 32 acres of uncultivated land in his field facing north free from all debts and demands which are owing to me or my heirs...together with 60 quarters of salt yearly taken from his salt-works at Fulstow... so that neither I the aforesaid Leo nor my heirs can demand anything against the aforesaid things on any occasion concerning debts which the aforesaid Ralph or his heirs ever owed us...'

It appears that Ralph de Bolebec had borrowed money from Leo of Lincoln, putting up some of his Levisham land as security. Malton

---

[5] a contract between Jews and Christians

Priory took on the repayment of the debt in return for the land. This was a common practice in Yorkshire, enabling religious houses to get access to land, facilitated by Jewish financiers. The word 'grant' in the charter does not mean 'gift'. What appears to be a transaction between two parties in fact involved three, the pious terminology presenting the acceptable face of the transaction.[6] Levisham mill as well as meadows and arable land near it were similarly held by Malton Priory for a time in a transaction involving Aaron son of Josce of York.

It is not clear how long the Malton Canons kept the Dundale grange, the mill and the other Levisham land. There are no documents relating to it after the mid-thirteenth century, and the Prior of Malton was not paying tax in Levisham in the 1301 Lay Subsidy, though still paying on land in Lockton and Newton.[7] By that date the peak of the boom in wool had passed. Was the Levisham grange no longer profitable? Was it a bit too remote for the kind of supervision the Gilbertines liked to exercise? Was it leased to other tenants, or did it revert to the manorial lord? There are many unanswered questions.

Bolebec's dealings with the Malton canons were not always entirely amicable. There are three documents relating to disputes about his unlawful taking of animals. At a meeting at Howe Bridge, between Malton and Pickering in 1239, Ralph took an oath on the Bible and agreed to pay compensation of 100 shillings sterling, two witnesses adding their signatures to the document as sureties. On another occasion there was a dispute relating to the woods of Horcome when again Bolebec was fined. However, his relations with the Priory were good enough for him to be granted:

> *'...perpetual and honourable sustenance with two horses and two men to minister to him as often as he comes to us and for as long as he wished to make the journey...'*

which must have been a useful staging post on his travels between Fulstow in Lincolnshire and Levisham.

---

[46] Richardson ch.5

[7] Yorks. Lay Subsidies

Chapter 7:
'William Watson, my Curate'
The role of church and priest in village life 1066-1700

The font in which generations of Levisham villagers were christened, once in St Mary's and now in the present Parish Church

CHRONOLOGY

1529-36	Reformation Parliament: carried out break with Rome
1535	Valor Ecclesiasticus: assessment of value of all benefices
1537	Pilgrimage of Grace: protest against changes in church
1549	Edward VI: Cranmer's 1st Prayer Book (ultra-Protestant)
1554	Reconciliation with Rome under Mary
1559	Elizabeth I's religious settlement (attempting compromise)
1642-9	Civil War: religion one issue
1649-60	Puritanism in ascendant during Commonwealth and Protectorate
1660	Restoration of monarchy
1689	Toleration Act: freedom of worship for protestant dissenters

SOURCES

On the ground	Documentary
Church buildings	Lists of incumbents
	Lay Subsidy lists
	Wills
	Church documents: Institution Act Books, Visitation Returns, Court Books

Background

In medieval England, religion was not a matter of private choice and individual belief, but a community affair, church and state jointly exercising a divinely ordained authority over the whole population of a Christian nation. At grass root level, civil power was exercised by the manorial lord, religious authority by the parish priest who was part of a whole army of clerics estimated to have numbered in the thirteenth century about one per cent of the population.[1]

The term '*clericus*', 'clerk', covered a whole array of men with at least a smattering of education that enabled them to read and write Latin – the language both of church and of government. As well as those who were ordained as deacons or priests, men we recognise

---

[1] Powick

today as 'clergymen' or 'clerks in holy orders', there was a far greater number in what were termed 'minor orders', on the fringes of the priesthood. Amongst those whom we would recognise as 'clergy', not all held the title to a benefice, and in most parishes the priest would have the assistance of at least one other '*clericus*'. Titles were sometimes used less precisely than today, so that the incumbent of Levisham is, in local documents such as wills, referred to variously as 'rector', 'pastor', 'chaplain', 'curate' (= 'having the *cure* or care of souls'), priest.

Initially, when a manorial lord provided a church its priest was his appointee, his 'man', whose particular job was not ploughing of the land or grinding of the grain but performing the rituals that marked the seasons of the year and the seasons of human life. As time went on, ecclesiastical control over the clergy by the bishop was strengthened at the expense of the local proprietor, but the parish priests of rural villages tended to remain very much local men, on the same level and with the same background and interests as most of their flock, required only to be sufficiently literate to be able to read the services.[2] In spite of attempts by the church hierarchy to encourage celibacy amongst the clergy, until the thirteenth century most parish priests were married and sometimes livings would pass from father to son.

Originally, the priest in charge of a parish was the *rector*, the position he occupied a *rectory*. He was supported partly out of the tithes (a contribution of a tenth of all produce from the inhabitants of the parish), partly from an endowment of land by the founder of the church, the glebe, and partly from fees and offerings from his parishioners. During the thirteenth century it became common for proprietors to donate a benefice to a monastery which then owned the greater tithes and held the right of appointment of the incumbent, known thereafter as a *vicar*, (that is, someone acting 'vicariously' for the rector).[3] The Rector then received the Great (or Rectoral) Tithes, levied on crops – everything growing directly from the land, the Vicar the Small (or Vicarial) Tithes on stock and animal products such as wool and eggs. This was not only a smaller amount, usually about one

---

[2] Bettey ch 2

[3] After the Reformation, monastic estates might be acquired by laymen who became Lay Rectors of churches.

third of the total, but also involved the produce most difficult to keep track on and collect. On the whole, it was the smaller, less wealthy parishes such as Levisham, less of a prize to a monastic house, that remained as rectories. Some indication of the wealth of a parish can be gained from the valuation carried out on the eve of the Reformation, the *Valor Ecclesiasticus;* Levisham, valued at £7 8s, was one of the poorer parishes in the area.

The duties of a parish priest in the diocese of York were set out in 1020 in the Law of Northumbrian Priests. There were the regular duties in church, ringing the bell and singing the services; observing the many festivals and fasts of the Christian year which provided welcome holidays ('holy days'). Every year in Holy Week they were to collect the holy oil that was used in baptism. They were enjoined to set an example by their style of life, for example not to frequent taverns. There was no mention of preaching, which was a post-Reformation emphasis. Their parishioners would be expected to be able to recite the Creed, the Lord's Prayer, the Ave Maria, to identify the sacraments, the seven deadly sins, seven virtues, the works of charity and acts of mercy.[4] Pictures on the walls of churches, like those painted round the nave of Pickering church in the fifteenth century, were visual aids conveying as much as the written word, depicting Bible stories, lives of the saints. They served to inculcate a sense of the arduous path to be followed by those hoping to escape the fires of hell and reach the bliss of heaven.

The priest was an integral part of every community, the ceremonials over which he presided intimately bound up with every aspect of life from birth to death.

Levisham

The earliest priest traced in Levisham records is named not in a church document but in the list of property owned by Ralph de Bolebec at the time of his death in an Inquisition Post Mortem dated 1252.[5] After detailing his land, its extent, value and from whom it was held, the inquisition continues: '*Patron of the church at Levisham of which*

---

[4] Swanson p. 271   [5] Calendar of Inquisitions

Robert le Bel is rector, worth 8 marks by the year'. Here is an example of the way in which a church and its priest were viewed as part and parcel of the assets of a manor, possessions with a financial tag attached.

A century later, and the rector, this time unnamed, appears again in a secular document, as a tax-payer of the Lay Subsidy in 1327: '*Rector Ecclesie:* iis' (Rector of the Church: 2s)*,* followed by: '*Johanne clerico: xiid*'. (John the Clerk: 12d).[6] From the same period come references to Levisham clergy in the records of the Forest Courts, confirming the presence of two clerics in the village, one who is referred to variously as 'rector', 'chaplain', 'parson', the other as 'clerk'. Sometimes they are in court standing bail for an offender, sometimes they are answering charges themselves of poaching or unlawfully taking timber.[7] They were poor men, who like many of their parishioners not above helping themselves to game and wood on occasions. From references to 'Thomas, son of John the Clerk of Levisham' we assume that some at least were married. The name 'Story' keeps appearing amongst names of rectors, the name of a farming family in Newtondale over several centuries, so presumably very local men. In 1336 John, parson of Levisham, is named, '*said to be the son of Ralph Story*'.[8] John Story, rector of Levisham, was a beneficiary under the will of William Chapman of Levisham in 1428; Adam Story, parson of Levisham, was a witness of several wills during the 1540's – indication of the close links between clergy and local community. Other incumbents have names that show they came from a bit further afield: Stephen de Hambleton, Lawrence de Northallerton, Richard de Aislaby[9] – all places within a forty-mile radius of Levisham.

Levisham people in the early years of the fourteenth century would no doubt be aware of the eccentric activities of a young man from Thornton Dale: Richard Rolle. Born in 1300, his early promise brought him to the attention of the Archdeacon of Durham who was instrumental in his entry at the age of fourteen to Oxford University.

[6] NRR IV. 142
[7] NRR IV
[8] NRR II. 114
[9] York Minster Library

After a few years, he dropped out without completing the seven year course, came home and, dressed in a habit made from his sisters' dresses, embarked on life as a hermit somewhere in the area. There is a suggestion that he had some association with Levisham: a nineteenth century writer, recalling her childhood in Levisham, referred to a well known locally as 'Rollo' which she connected with Richard Rolle.[10]

The names 'Roll Spring' and 'Roll Wood', (now spelt 'Rowle'), could have derived from association with the hermit Rolle. He went on to become an early writer in the English language, translating parts of the Bible into English; he was a passionate exponent of an understanding of religion as inner experience rather than either an intellectual discipline or an observation of forms and rituals. He went on to live in Hampole, near Doncaster, and whilst this is the place to which his life can be definitively linked, his formative years were spent in the area around Pickering , and bear witness to a serious interest amongst ordinary people in the exploration of religious ideas.

Wills provide insight into religious attitudes and practices. Pre-Reformation wills usually start with a commendation of the soul to God and St Mary or other saints. They then go on to detail money bequeathed to the church, using the formula *'for forgotten tithes'*, sometimes leaving additional sums *'for the repair of the body of the church'*. In the earliest surviving Levisham will (1428), William Chapman, a man of some substance, left money to various religious bodies in the area – the cathedral of York, the Friars Mendicant of Scarborough, the Guild of St Christopher and six Guilds in Pickering and Whitby. These were the local charities to be remembered by a pious man in his will. Several men including the parish priest, Henry Botham (1467) expressed a wish to be buried within the church: *'before the sacrament'*, (John Fairweather 1546), *'within the church at the end of the stall where I used to sit'* (William Rede 1562). In a number of these early wills, a bequest was made to the priest with a request for his prayers for their soul. This is where we meet *'William Watson, my curate...'*, his prayers requested by several of his flock. It is the same William Watson we have met before, having a brush with the law over

---

[10] Beatrice Walker: The Well of Life. 13.

his poaching activities. He was in trouble a few years later when he was accused of '*keeping Elizabeth Readshawe, wife of Robert Readshawe of Filey, suspiciously in his house…*',[11] but any irregularities in his conduct did not invalidate his intercessory role. One parishioner left him twelve pence, another his best lamb to be taken on the feast of St Peter, another a wether, '*to pray for me*'. The Reformation discouraged this preoccupation with death and challenged the teaching about purgatory that had been a characteristic of late medieval piety; from 1562, Levisham wills record no more legacies to the church or requests for prayers after death. Instead, bequests were encouraged to help the living – the poor and needy.

During the fourteenth and fifteenth century, a popular form of piety was to subscribe to the provision for a chantry-priest who would be attached to a parish church but whose main duty was prayer for the souls of the deceased. When chantries were dissolved under Henry VIII's Reformation legislation, the revenues attached to one of the Pickering chantries, the Lady Guild, were used to found a grammar school with the former chantry-priest, Richard Judson, as schoolmaster on a salary of £1.15s a year.[12] A century later, a Richard Judson was vicar of Middleton and then rector of Levisham: a descendent, perhaps, of the chantry-priest-turned-schoolmaster?

Following the Dissolution of the Monasteries, some of the evicted monks were found employment as parish priests. A former monk from Whitby, John Watson, became rector of Levisham in 1571. He, it was said, '*read English distinctly, seemed zealous, and had abjured papistry*'.[13] The use of English instead of Latin was part of a new emphasis on the importance of understanding alongside ritual observances. We have nothing to indicate how the new form of English service was received by the congregation. There is no record of recusants (Catholics who refused to conform) in Levisham; any who were unhappy with the changes that were being made kept their opinions to themselves. The savage retribution meted out by Henry VIII's government to the leaders of the protest march led by

[11] Cross and Vickers
[12] Chantry certs
[13] Cross & Vickers

Yorkshiremen, known as the Pilgrimage of Grace, would have sent out a warning against publicly voicing dissent – safer to conform, and keep your private beliefs to yourself.

Nor is there record of non-conformists from the puritan wing, an increasingly influential section of the church in Elizabethan times and after. A reference in a Visitation Return of 1663 to Richard Judson being reprimanded for not wearing a surplice may indicate that he had puritan leanings.[14] Quakerism took root in England during the Protectorate; there were a number of Quakers in Lockton in the 1680's, but none recorded in Levisham.[15] Perhaps the dissenting tradition in Lockton, evident in the strength of Methodism in the nineteenth century, is related to the absence of a resident parish priest (Lockton being a Chapelry of the Parish of Middleton), and goes back to this period. In 1662, two years after the Restoration, the Levisham churchwardens were instructed to see to repairs to the church and purchase of books and 'other ornaments'[16] which perhaps suggests the dislocation of normal church life during the Commonwealth years.

The 'living' provided for a priest included land, (the glebe land) and a house. Fuller information about both land and house emerge from the Church Terriers from the late seventeenth century onwards. The only information about the house from this earlier period is the censuring of George Hicks, (instituted rector in 1621) for *'suffering the thatch to be blown off from part of the housing belonging to the parsonage and not repairing it'*.[17] In Richard Judson's time (1661-66), the house was

A Good Read

The Voices of Morebath   The Stripping of the Altars. Traditional Religion in England c.1400 – c.1570. Eamon Duffy. (Yale Uni. Press 2001)
Based on the meticulously kept and annotated account book of the parish priest of a small Devon village, the author reconstructs the process of change during the period of the Reformation that battered the securities of religious traditions that had underpinned social life for centuries.

---

[14] Borth. Visitation returns

[15] Borthwick: Court Books 1682 & 1685

[16] Borthwick:Court Bk 1662

[17] Borthwick:Court Bk 1641

one of only three in the village with more than one hearth, he and two others in the village paying Hearth Tax on two hearths.

There is a list of Levisham rectors painted on a board in the porch of the present church. Most of them can never be anything more than names to us, a succession of men who maintained both the fabric of the church (the Rector was responsible for the chancel), and its spiritual heritage during centuries when religion could be either a cohesive or a divisive force within a community.

Chapter 8 :
Thomas Sowerby, Constable
Looking after Parish affairs 16th-19th centuries

A page from the 1662 Hearth Tax return for Levisham. The first line reads: 'Richard Judson of Levisham, clerk hath Two Harths' © Crown Copyright

CHRONOLOGY

16th C	Manorial Court superseded by Parish Vestry as body responsible for village affairs
1555, 1691	Highways Acts
1563, 1597, 1601	Poor Law Acts.
1834	Poor Law Amendment Act
1894	Local Government Act: Parish, Rural District Councils

SOURCES

	Documentary
Quarter Session reports	N.Riding Record Soc.
Levisham Vestry Minutes 1794 - 1899	NYCRO
Levisham Churchwarden's Account Book	NYCRO

Background

From the thirteenth century onwards, the feudal manor and the Court Leet through which it operated declined in importance. The old aristocracy, 'overmighty subjects' who with their castles and armies of retainers had challenged the power of the monarchy, was decimated during the Wars of the Roses. The Tudors looked for support from the up-and-coming class of landed country gentry, who in their role as Justices of the Peace were given a greater part than before in local administration. Under Tudor legislation, the parish through its Vestry meeting acquired new responsibilities. The monarch, now head of the church, used the ecclesiastical structures that were already in place for the secular function of local government, church and state tightly bound together from the top to the grassroots of society. The unpaid offices of Constable, Overseers of the Poor, Surveyor of Highways, joined the Churchwardens, all appointed annually by the Vestry and operating under the jurisdiction of the Justices of the Peace. The office of Churchwarden was the most ancient amongst the parish officials, dating back to at least the twelfth century. They were the 'guardians' of the parish church, always men of some standing in the community, able to command the respect that would enable them to exercise the authority vested in them. The Parish had a statutory duty to maintain its roads, the Surveyor organising working parties from all the householders who were required to give six days' labour a year or pay a fine of twelve pence a day. The Constable was responsible for law and order, and also for the collection of any national taxes. The Overseers of the Poor also handled public funds, collecting and distributing the Poor Rate. All these men were in trouble at the next Quarter Sessions if they were found to be 'neglecting their office'.

The North Riding Quarter Sessions were held, as their name implies, four times a year, meeting in rotation in different parts of the region, usually Thirsk, Richmond, Helmsley and Malton. On January 11th 1619, for example, The Quarter Sessions were held at Malton presided over by Christopher Mitchell, gentleman, Deputy for the High Sheriff. The nine Justices present included Sir Richard Etherington of Ebberston who was at that time Steward of Pickering Castle and held the Manors of Levisham, Lockton and Goathland as well as Ebberston. The panels of jurymen drawn mainly from the yeoman class included William Dobson, yeoman, of Levisham.[1]

Theft was the most common offence to be brought before the Justices – on this occasion, they dealt with the theft of a ewe valued at nine shillings and a pound of red wool worth four pence. A few years earlier, Matilda Wilkinson, spinster, of Thornton was found guilty of stealing a pair of stockings (3d) a petticoat (4d) and a neckerchief (3d) for which she was to be whipped in Malton, *'and from thence conveyed from Constable to Constable'* in the parishes through which she had to pass on her way *'...to Thornton, there to be whipped upon a holyday after evening prayer time from the church stile to the place of her late dwelling there.'*[2] As well as criminal offences, the Quarter Sessions dealt with a range of civil matters, for example recusancy, the licensing of Alehouses, the maintenance of bastard children. They oversaw the condition of roads and bridges: Howe Bridge, on the road between Malton and Pickering, was observed in 1607/8 to be *'in great decay and if not presently repaired will require a great sum of money'*. It was decided

[1] NRR Soc. vol II [2] NRR Soc. vol I. 101

that a rate of £6.13.4. be levied[3] – a task for the parish road surveyors. The scale of wages for labourers was kept under review. In 1658, carpenters, masons and thatchers were the highest paid workers, earning twelve pence a day ('without meat'). A farm worker received £4 a year, on top of his board and keep – twice as much as a cook or dairy maid.[4]

Although neither the term 'democracy' nor the idea of a universal right of participation in decision-making through local or national elections were to gain acceptance as political ideals until the nineteenth century, from the sixteenth century onwards members of local communities were exercising considerable responsibility in the running of their towns and villages. There was no national police force to maintain law and order; no Inland Revenue office to administer national taxation, (which was looked on as an occasional levy to cope with unusual events such as wars rather than a regular income needed to run public services). The system of local administration that was developed during the late fifteenth and sixteenth centuries seems to have worked satisfactorily in the typical small, cohesive village communities of the day. New systems were needed in the urban, industrial society that was emerging during the eighteenth and nineteenth century.

Levisham

In the year 1664, the Constable of Levisham submitted his return for the collection of the Hearth Tax for the village. This was a tax of two shillings per hearth levied between the years 1662 and 1689 payable by all except the poorest households. The returns, listing the householders by name with the number of hearths in each dwelling, are an invaluable source of information for local historians. The Levisham return listed thirty-two households, all with one hearth except for the Parsonage where Richard Judson had two hearths, and the two-hearth home of Robert Paite. At the end of the form was a note: '*These are to testify that the house of Ann Browne which formerly paid Hearth Money was last winter consumed with fire and not yet rebuilt*'. It was

[3] ibid p.238   [4] NRR Soc. vol VI. 3

signed by the incumbent, Richard Judson, Matthew Adamson, Churchwarden and Thomas Sowerby, Constable. Here we have a glimpse of local government in action, and one of the earliest records of the names of two of the village officials. What sort of people were these men who managed village affairs – men such as Matthew Adamson and Thomas Sowerby?

'Sowerby' is not a surname that occurs often in Levisham records. No Sowerby wills have been found; nothing to indicate the presence of a Sowerby family in the village for an extended period. Almost all we know comes from the Parish Registers: the meagre facts that in 1675 Thomas Sowerby married Elizabeth Bayley, member of a long-established Levisham family, and that two years later their daughter Jane was christened. By the time of his marriage he was already a person of some standing in the village – Constable in 1664, a Churchwarden in 1667 when he signed the Bishop's Transcripts; by 1673 he was paying tax for two hearths – apparently upwardly mobile. It seems reasonable to infer that he came to Levisham as a young man, lived and worked there for around fifteen years, getting established, starting a family, doing well, and then moved on. A likely guess is that he was a blacksmith – like the miller, a trade that was always in demand in a farming village. The office of Constable often fell to the smith because his duties called for a fit, strong man. An investigation into patterns of mobility in the population of Levisham[5] between the sixteenth and nineteenth centuries has shown in the earlier part of the period a core of stable, settled farming families, with more mobile men following a trade or craft coming in, moving out, leaving only a small trace in the village records. Sowerby was such a man.

Matthew Adamson, the Churchwarden whose name appears at the end of the 1664 Hearth Tax return, was a member of one of the more substantial farming families (by Levisham standards), traceable in the village from early in the seventeenth century until the time of the Enclosure (1770). He represents one of the 'core families' in the community, those with a stake in the land, men who in their wills described themselves as 'yeomen'.

[5] Halse

To move on a century: the Minutes of the Levisham Vestry Meetings between 1794 and 1899 survive,[6] recording the annual meeting held in the old Chapel of Ease until it fell into ruin around 1850, then in the School. The main business was the appointment of the officers for the next year: two Churchwardens, two Overseers of the Poor, a Constable and his deputy, two Road Surveyors and two Land Tax Collectors to deal with the Parish contribution to the fixed tax quota for the county. As with the Hearth tax, the Land Tax returns (available between 1780 and 1832 in the NYCRO) are a useful source of information about the population of a village, naming owners and occupiers of property along with their tax assessment. Levisham was liable for a payment of just over twenty pounds, amounting to about four pence per acre, shared out amongst thirty owners or occupiers of whom seven paid over half of the total. These men, the more substantial farmers, figure largely in the lists of office-holders – men like Jeremiah Pickering, a tenant farmer who first appears in village records in 1796 as one of the Land Tax collectors. Two years later he served as an Overseer of the Poor, in 1800 he was Churchwarden for two years, then was collecting taxes again in 1805. During this time he and his wife Mary had four children whose baptisms are recorded. They then disappear from the records, but Jeremiah's name figures in the Pickering Tithe Award of 1838. He was perhaps following a pattern that can be found at this period of getting a start by leasing a relatively small farm at Levisham, then moving on to greener pastures. There are few names of the earlier long-standing Levisham families in these lists. Even families making their living from the land had become much more mobile than previously, so men were pressed into taking their share in running the village soon after they arrived, before they upped and moved on.

As part of the ecclesiastical system, vestry meetings were held under the chairmanship of the incumbent – the one person who at the beginning of the period could be guaranteed to be literate and had an official standing in the place; someone likely to stay in the parish for many years and who would continue to be a key figure in village affairs until the twentieth century.

---

[6] NYCRO Mic. 2424

Chapter 9:
Three Centuries of Yeoman Farmers
16th to 18th centuries

Above the hearth, the centre of family life, would hang the iron cooking pot on its reckon.

LEVISHAM: A CASE STUDY IN LOCAL HISTORY

CHRONOLOGY

Some national events that would have affected village life:-

1529 – 39	Reformation
1588	Spanish Armada
1642-6	Civil War
1649-60	Commonwealth and Protectorate
1660	Restoration of monarchy

SOURCES

On the ground	Documentary
Ryedale Folk Museum	Wills
Beck Isle Museum	Parish Registers
	Hearth Tax lists
	Muster Rolls

From the sixteenth century onwards, there is more documentation relating to the daily lives of ordinary people. This chapter is based mainly on wills. A series of wills from one place over a period of years provides insight into the social and economic structure of the community, the occupations of its inhabitants, the range of income represented there. It is possible to reconstruct some of the families, view their homes and treasured possessions and observe their progress through the generations.

Until 1858, wills were proved in ecclesiastical courts, and wills for the province of York before that date are to be found in the Borthwick Institute, York.

At Ryedale Folk Museum, Hutton-le-Hole, typical houses from the surrounding area dating from different periods have been reconstructed, from which it is possible to get a vivid impression of the setting for everyday domestic life – how people cooked, where they slept, washed, went to the toilet. Stang End, a yeoman's house from Danby, has been re-erected there, its furnishing backed up by research into the family who lived there in the early eighteenth century.

Levisham families

Over eighty Levisham wills have been researched, the earliest dated 1428 but most from the mid-sixteenth to the end of the eighteenth century. These are the wills of people with a solid stake, however small, in their society – a stake they want to protect and hand on. In them we meet families whose stake was increasing over the years, the sums of money in their bequests rising from pence to pounds, their furniture and their flocks expanding. They were, however, without exception, 'small' people of modest means, their living derived mainly from their sheep. There would also be people in the village who did not leave wills, people with little in the way of material possessions to leave behind them; the wills cannot be assumed to cover the whole range of village society; the picture they give is incomplete.

When the wills give the occupation of the testator it is usually 'husbandman', sometimes 'labourer' which did not at that time have the nineteenth century connotation of an underclass of low-paid workers, but denoted someone working on land he did not own: a farmer's son, for example. The term 'yeoman', which appears first in the Levisham wills in 1613, seems to bear a similar meaning to 'husbandman', implying ownership of his land. There are wills of a carpenter, a tailor, a weaver and a miller: these the only four whose living was not derived entirely from the land, and of them only one will, made by William Dobson the tailor, does not include some land.

There is only one person amongst these Levisham testators who is styled 'gentleman'. It is a term that is hard to define with any precision but denotes a status that would have been recognised within that society. 'Gentility' was often related to the ownership of land and exercise of jurisdiction that went with it, but covered also members of professions such as lawyers, doctors, clergymen. From the sixteenth century onwards the gentry class grew – people who were upwardly-mobile, increasingly influential in the conduct of public affairs.[1] William Poad (will 1734) is termed 'gentleman'. He was the head of

---

[1] See Heal & Holmes: The Gentry in England and Wales

the senior branch of the Poad family – a family that can be traced in Levisham records from the sixteenth to the nineteenth centuries, its members designated 'yeoman' or 'husbandman' in previous wills. He, one presumes, claimed the title of 'gentleman' when he acquired the lordship of the manor of Levisham at some date between 1716 (when it was held by Thomas Etherington of Ebberston)[2] and 1770 when his son, another William Poad, is named Lord of the Manor in the Enclosure Award. The bequests in Poad's will do not suggest any change in his material situation from his yeoman predecessors. He left an oxgang of land in the open fields to each of his two sons who divided his seven closes between them and each inherited a house in the village. The remainder of his 2000-year lease was mortgaged for £100: did he mortgage his estate to enable him to buy the manor? Was he, one wonders, more interested in raising his social status than in the soundness of his financial position?

Of the thirty households listed in the 1673 Hearth Tax returns, eleven bear the names of 'core families' who can be traced in village records generation after generation. According to this list, there were only two households with more than a single hearth, both of these with two hearths. There was no recording of any households exempted from the tax on account of poverty; the one person noted as not paying the tax was Anne Browne, paying for one hearth in 1662, but missing from the list in 1664 because her house *'was last winter consumed with fire and not yet rebuilt'*. These tax returns suggest a community of a fairly uniform, fairly lowly economic status.

The number of households has remained remarkably constant over the centuries. From the information gained from wills, at least sixteen households can be identified in the mid-sixteenth century, at least twenty-seven by the end of the century (the number more to do with additional information rather than additional people). In the Hearth Tax returns of the second half of the seventeenth century, households numbered between thirty and thirty-four, similar to the range of twenty-one to thirty-four households recorded in the nineteenth century censuses, a consistency likely to be related to the

[2] VCH.p 451

number of families that could be maintained from the acreage of cultivable land.

The 1848 Tithe Award with its accompanying map shows the exact lay-out of Levisham, the houses, barns, garths, as well as the fields. While the houses have been repeatedly altered and rebuilt over the years, the likelihood is that the house-plots and their boundaries have stayed the same. Unfortunately for the historian trying to trace links with the past, house and field names keep changing. Of the houses named in the sixteenth to eighteenth century wills, only two can be definitely identified. Kidstye House in Newtondale, named in Peter Fairweather's will in 1641 still has the same name today, and the name variously spelt as 'Roll' and 'Rowl' figures in the will of Richard Poad in 1668, in the property of John Poad in the Tithe Award and can be traced through the deeds of various property transactions down the centuries to the present day.

Levisham was a small and intimate community. From wills and Parish Registers we can trace intermarriage between village families, Read with White, Poad with Read, Read with Consett. The same names keep recurring as Churchwardens: Adamson, Hewitson, Darrell, Baley. The same names turn up as well in the church Court Books in the late seventeenth century,[3] people who were reported for fornication, for not attending church, not paying their church assessment. In such a small place everyone would know everyone else and be aware of their neighbour's circumstances and know who was in need. Although there is little evidence of extreme poverty, there would always be individuals, particularly widows, in difficult circumstances. Their need is recognised in the wills which include a bequest to 'the poor of the parish'. James Adamson (1628) left five shillings to the poor of the parish, specifying that it was to be distributed to four widows whom he named, two to receive two shillings each, two six pence. William Hewitson (1645) left 13s 4d for the overseers of the poor to distribute at their discretion. Tuke, writing at the end of the eighteenth century about agriculture in the North Riding, applauded the 'honourable spirit of independence …

[3] Borthwick Institute

in the breast of the lower orders'.[4] We get the impression that these bequests to the poor were given in the spirit of neighbourly goodwill, not condescension.

There is little evidence of contacts outside a very limited geographical area. Names appear of relatives, friends, business connections in neighbouring villages and in the nearby towns of Pickering, Whitby and Malton. The bachelor Jacob Read (1714) had the most far-flung circle of contacts, remembering in his will friends in Marishes, Whitby and Helmsley, but can we have much hope that his niece Elizabeth *'at London'*, whose husband's name he did not know, ever received her legacy of one shilling?

There are a few intriguing references to disputes and undercurrents of ill feeling. What, for example, was behind Peter Storey's stipulation (1573) that his wife was not to marry again *'without the consent of my trustie friends Richard Postgate, J. Read, Francis Wilkinson, except she avoyde my tenement'*? William Read's will (1692) left instructions for the shared management between his wife and son of *'that estate which is now in contest'*.

Wills help to indicate family size. Levisham Parish Registers do not start until 1600, and are fragmentary until the eighteenth century, but assuming that most wills include a bequest to all surviving children, the twenty-two sixteenth century families leaving wills had an average of four children. In the next century, the average size of the families represented in the thirty-two wills had dropped to three. Without Parish Registers there is no way of knowing accurately the statistics of mortality, but we realise in reading the wills that a number of them were made by relatively young men whose expectation of premature death may have been their reason for making the will – setting their affairs in order for the sake of their family. Thomas Read (1567) made provision for the guardianship of his children; Peter Storey (1573) left money for the bringing up of his children until his eldest son was of age; John Darrell (1586) left 12d each to four friends *'to stand godfathers and friends to my children'*. George White (1591) and Thomas Wardle (1613) both had under age children; William Darrell

[4] Tuke.p 314

(1654) and Thomas Bayley (1659) both had unmarried daughters under 21, while Thomas Clarke (1654) died without children but with the possibility that his wife was pregnant.

In the earlier wills from the sixteenth century clothes figure significantly amongst the bequests, a man naming who should have his jackets, doublet and hose, cape, hat; a woman her gown and girdle. It is an indication of the level at which people were then living that even 'one leather doublet, being my worst doublet' (John Reed, 1587) was worth handing on. A century later, clothes were given an estimated value in inventories – *'purse and apparel: £3'* (Richard Consett, 1706) but were no longer significant enough to be distributed amongst families and friends. The last clothing bequest was in 1645 when William Hewitson left his new coat to one friend, a suit of his best clothes to another and the rest of his clothes to a third.

Household linen was often included amongst the bequests: blankets, bed sheets of linen and hemp, coverlets, feather pillows, bed curtains, mattresses. The most frequently mentioned item of furniture was the chest or 'ark'; some households had several – Peter Storey (1573) left 'my great ark' to one son, 'the chest that stands under the window' to another and 'the little chest' to a daughter. Beds are mentioned, tables –'table boards' implying trestle tables; there would be a form or chairs; cupboards or 'aumbries' appear more rarely. A brass pot was an item of value in some of the early wills; by the mid-seventeenth century pewter had made an appearance, with a pewter dubler (large plate) something to prize.

From the eighteenth century wills which have an inventory attached we learn something about the house as well as its contents. A typical Levisham house had two downstairs rooms, the forehouse, a general living room furnished with table, chairs and chest where there was the hearth with its reckon on which hung the cooking pot, and the parlour which contained beds. Sometimes there was also an upstairs chamber. According to his inventory (1699), Peter Storey's house in Newtondale had a kitchen in addition containing '*1 old spoon, 1 kimlin* (wooden trough for kneading dough)*, 1 churn with small implements'*. Such are the houses that figure in wills, but remembering that wills are likely to be made by the better-off members of society, they may not have been typical for the village as a whole. Writing in 1800 about the North Riding generally, Tuke describes the typical labourer's cottage as a 'hovel' consisting of one small room, likely to be damp and *'very unwholesome…'*,[5] in which all the living, cooking, sleeping took place.

A few of the sixteenth century wills include reference to weapons and armour. These were years when, with the threat of foreign invasion, the government required Muster Rolls to be made listing all men between 16 and 60 who were able to equip themselves with weapons and be available to fight if needed. A Muster Roll for the Pickering Lyth Wapentake for 1539[6] lists the Levisham men, archers and bilmen who could provide *'horse and harness'*, and those (a longer list) who could present their person, but *'without harness'*. The 'harness' referred to was basic fighting gear: a 'sallet' or helmet, and a 'jack' — a leather or canvas jerkin covered with small iron plates.[7] Thomas Storey's will (1541) includes a sallet; James Dobson (1557) left a sword and dagger, George Wilkinson (1562) two helmets and a halbert — a long-handled, axe-like weapon.

But the real wealth of a family was not in the house but outside. It was, first of all, in the land itself, including a share in the three open fields, Braygate Field, Limpseygate Field and Little Field, as well as various enclosed fields or closes and rights on the commons. When Thomas Prestman (1541) bequeathed to his son *'one oxgang of corn through the fields'*, he was passing on his share in the three open arable fields of the village. The 'oxgang' was a measure based originally on what could be cultivated in one year by one ox, the acreage varying according to the quality of the land. In Levisham, an oxgang appears to have been about twelve acres. In these references we are encountering the traditional way of farming when each man's ox joined an eight-ox team, capable of ploughing a carucate (= eight oxgangs) in a year, sharing in the communally organised working of the arable land. Some wills refer to the crops grown: barley, oats,

---

[5] Tuke: Agriculture in the North Riding p.41
[6] PRO E 36/23
[7] PRO Information Leaflet

wheat and rye. After 1585, a new phrase appears in wills: *'my title and term of years in my tenement in Levisham, by grant of Sir Henry Gates…'*. After this date, land features more prominently in wills as men ensure that the title to their land is passed on to their heirs. Gates, an important figure in the political life of North Yorkshire, held the manor of Levisham for a few years between 1585 and 1589, during which time he granted 2000-year leases to the tenant farmers – leases which continued until legislation in 1891 made it possible to convert them into freeholds.

Numerous 'closes' or 'intacks' had over the years been taken from what had once been part of the Forest. Some names indicate their usage – 'Calf Close', 'Lamb Close', 'Far Corn Close', some recall previous owners – 'Mitchell Close', 'Robinson Brow', some relate to the type of land, like the Ings on the marshy land by the beck, and various Haggs on the wooded slopes along Newtondale and on the slopes above the Ings by the beck side. The various references to *'newly acquired closes'* give the impression of a brisk market in land. The closes included pasture, grassland and woodland. A few wills give instructions about the management of the woodland; John Adamson (1628) willed that his son Anthony *'shall not fell any wood in Great Park Sike neither oak nor ash nor crabtree till he become 21 years, except for building a house'*. William Pate's woodland (1712) was to be shared between his three sons, one of them, William, *'to have liberty to choose five of the best trees'*.

Sheep were the most valuable part of the livestock. The listed bequests of one or more lambs to a string of relatives and friends were made by people who counted their wealth in sheep. Out of eighty wills, over half specifically mention sheep; where there is an inventory, in all cases but one the sheep are the largest item in the balance sheet, the exception being George Featherstone (1720) whose cattle were valued at £14 as against £10 for his sheep. Most people kept a few cows; when they are named, like William Pate's *'a cow called Nuttie'* (1712), you have a sense that these were friends of the family, kept to supply their owners with milk, butter and cheese. There are a few wills from women, mainly widows, and most of them have a cow or two. Oxen and horses supplied traction power for the ploughs and harrows that figure amongst the *'implements of husbandry'*. Was there an accepted convention that pigs and poultry were excluded from the goods disposed of by will? Even hives of bees are accounted for but nowhere in the Levisham wills is there a mention of the pigs or poultry that must have been rooting around the farmsteads.

The typical homestead comprised the house with a garth behind and a barn and other outhouses adjoining where the husbandry gear was to be found: plough, harrow, yokes, carts. Ironware is singled out for special mention: *'a shackell with bolt of iron'*, *'nayles of iron'* (1562) various references to an *'iron-bound waine'*, *'all iron gear'* (1569), *'7 iron hoops'* for binding cart wheels (1699).

There are hints in the wills of the customs governing testamentary dispositions: references to the *'wife's third'*, and a *'child's portion'*. Usually the house and title to the land were left to the eldest son with the younger children receiving 'closes' and a share of household goods and livestock; occasionally the estate was divided, as in the will of William Pate (1712) when his holding of one and a half oxgangs in the Levisham fields was split between two of his three sons.

Two wills, one of William Pate (1712) and William Dickinson (1732) illustrate the range of income and possessions of Levisham husbandmen early in the eighteenth century.

There were Pates in Levisham throughout the seventeenth century, from the time of Richard Pate who was incumbent of the parish between 1582 and 1617. In the Hearth Tax Returns of 1662 and 1664 there were three Pate households, Robert Pate being one of the two two-hearth householders in the village. In 1673 there were two Pate families, one headed by a William – perhaps the William who died in 1712? He was Churchwarden in 1672, a responsible, office-holding member of the community. From his will, we have the impression of someone who was steadily building up his property, acquiring new closes, planning the development of his woodland with instructions to his sons about the felling of trees for ten years after his death. He must have believed that what he had to leave would support two of his sons; however, we discover from the Parish

Registers that both sons died within a few years of their father. His widow lived until 1730; she is the last Pate named in Levisham registers. William Pate and his wife Mary had three sons and a daughter, Jane, who was married first to a member of the Merry family of Lockton, and then to one of the Levisham Poads – both established yeoman families in the area. As well as his land in the arable fields, William had four closes two of which were referred to as *'newly taken up'*, three Ings, a *'little Intack on the west side of the town'* on the wooded slopes of Newtondale. According to his inventory, his most valuable asset was his sheep, valued at £34; his oxen and cattle were valued at £17.5s, horse £4.5s, corn £13.10s, husbandry gear £2, household goods £2.14s.4d, purse and apparel £2. There was £8.16s owing to him in outstanding debts, his total assets amounting to £84.5s.4d. In only one of the Levisham inventories do the testator's assets exceed this, reaching as much as £100.

If William Pate typifies the better-off Levisham yeoman farmer, William Dickinson represents the man at the lower end of the economic ladder. The name Dickinson does not go back as far in Levisham records as the name Pate, but there were Dickinsons, described as yeomen, from the 1730s. William Dickinson died in 1732. He does not appear to have had any children, but left to his wife his house and half-oxgang of land. The total assets in his inventory came to £24.15s.6d. Like Pate, his sheep were the most valuable item in his inventory, assessed at £10.10s. His house had two rooms; the listed furniture comprised one cupboard, one table, two chairs, two beds, one chest. There were miscellaneous cooking implements – reckon, iron pot, a pan, two pewter dishes. £4 was the sum total for all the household goods. He had a horse, one cow, and corn to the value of £3.2s.

From Pate to Dickinson, they were basically subsistence farmers, cultivating the land in a manner that was soon to become outdated as market forces impelled changes in farming practices.

Chapter 10: Issac Wykes and Robert Skelton

Village Parsons in the 18th & 19th centuries

St Mary's Church, Levisham, as it would have looked before the addition of the tower in 1897.

LEVISHAM: A CASE STUDY IN LOCAL HISTORY

CHRONOLOGY

National		Local	
1720's	Start of Methodist movement		
		1764	John Wesley in Pickering
		1797	1st Methodist Society in Lockton
		1801–2	St Mary's Levisham rebuilt
		1822	1st Methodist Chapel in Lockton
1833	Start of Tractarian (Oxford) Movement		
1851	Census of religious worship	1850	Levisham Chapel of Ease in disrepair
		1859	Primitive Methodist chapel in Levisham
		1884	Chapel of Ease rebuilt
		1887	Tower added to St Mary's

SOURCES (Levisham)

On the ground	Documentary	
Remains of St Mary's Church, and memorial tablets	Local newspapers	Libraries
Present Church, formerly Chapel of Ease	Herring Visitation (1743)	Borthwick
Former Primitive Methodist Chapel	Diocesan Returns 1865 and 1868	Borthwick
	Church Terriers	Borthwick
	Levisham Churchwardens' Accounts	NYCRO
	Methodist Circuit Plans	NYCRO

Sources are plentiful for anything relating to the church. York Diocesan documents, housed in the Borthwick Institute, York, include Visitation Returns covering enquiries by Bishops into the state of the parishes and Institution and Court Books with records of appointments, and disciplinary matters relating to clergy.

The main repository of Methodist archives is the John Rylands Library, Manchester. There are a few nineteenth century preaching plans in the NYCRO.

Background

After two centuries of bitter religious controversy with executions, burnings, persecution and eventually civil war, by the eighteenth century the intensity of religious passion had died down. Intellectual enquiry focussed on science; reason was valued above emotion and 'enthusiasm' was almost a term of abuse. A more tolerant attitude to religious differences prevailed, with the Toleration Act of 1689 opening the way for a greater acceptance of Protestant Dissenters (Quakers, Independents), though Catholics were still regarded with suspicion and the penal laws that prevented their holding any public office remained until 1829.

The Church of England fell into a comfortable lethargy. The right to nominate to church livings (*advowson*) was bought and sold like a piece of real estate,[1] often held by members of the landed gentry, creating that cosy relationship between parson and squire familiar to us from the pages of Jane Austen. Clergymen with an eye to maximising their income could hold more than one living (*pluralism*), employing curates to help with the performance of their clerical duties. There was no specific training for the clergy until the second half of the nineteenth century; ordination was at the discretion of the bishop. Most but not all the clergy were university graduates: in the diocesan records of ordinations, the non-graduates were noted as 'literate', recalling earlier centuries when literacy was rare, and a prime requirement of a clergyman was to read the services.

---

[1] see advertisements in local press, e.g. Yorkshire Gazette Feb 23 1856

The Methodist Movement started in the 1720's amongst a group of Anglican clergy attempting to revive their own church. By the end of the century it had become a separate body with its own internal divisions leading to the formation of various splinter groups. During the nineteenth century the distinctive architecture of non-conformist chapels became familiar in towns and villages throughout the land, with often a Wesleyan and a Primitive Methodist chapel in the same village. Within the Church of England, Evangelicals stimulated personal piety and drew attention to needs for social reform and Tractarians revived interest in tradition and ritual.

Levisham

Two names, but four people: Isaac Wykes I and II, father and son, followed by Robert Skelton I and II, also father and son, served Levisham as Rector for the greater part of two centuries, from the institution of Isaac Wykes I in 1698 to the death of Robert Skelton II in 1877. The first Isaac Wykes came from a clerical family, son of Marmaduke Wykes vicar of Ellerburn near Thornton Dale. Isaac, baptised in Pickering in 1673, graduated from Edinburgh University in 1691 and two years later at the age of twenty, was ordained Deacon in York. For the next four years he worked as a curate in the parishes of Amotherby and Appleton-le-Street before being ordained priest in 1697, shortly before succeeding Charles Collinson as rector of Levisham. With his wife Mary he moved into the Parsonage House which was to be his home for the rest of his life. One of his earliest entries in the Parish Registers recorded the baptism of their daughter Jael in 1701; their son, the Isaac who was to be his successor, was born twenty years later, the youngest of their six children. Their parsonage house, today's Rectory Farm, is mentioned in several Church Terriers, the fullest description in a Terrier of 1764:

'*The Parsonage House Fourteen yards long and six yards Broad, Built with stone and cover (sic) with Thatch, containing three Low Rooms, Two of which are floored with Stone, the other with Clay, and each of them Plastered with Lime. Three Chambers Floored with Bords and Plastered with Lime.*

One Barn twelve yards long and six yards broad, Built with Stone and covered with Thatch. One Beast House fourteen yards long and four yards Broad built with Stone and Covered with Thatch.'

During Wykes' incumbency, in 1743 Archbishop Herring's Visitation of the Diocese of York took place. The replies to the eleven questions asked by the Archbishop give a detailed picture of the complex patchwork of parish organisation in an age of pluralism. As well as holding the office of Rector of Levisham, Wykes was also from 1730 Vicar of Kirby Grindalyth, a village about twice the size of Levisham (according to the Visitation Return, forty families as against twenty in Levisham), a good twenty miles away to the south-east of Malton. To help him with the services in these two widely separated parishes, – one service with sermon every Sunday in each parish, the Sacrament three times a year, – he employed as Curate Thomas Deason, the Vicar of Middleton, which included Cropton and Lockton in its parish. Deason held a service in one of these three churches each week. Adding still further to the complication, Wykes acted as assistant curate at Ebberston and Allerston to Arthur Caley who lived at Robin Hood's Bay where he had charge of the chapelries of Ugglebarnby, Eskdale and Fylingthorpe. Caley was also Rector of Cowlam, a parish away on the Wolds east of Malton, where there was only one family, so little need for his ministrations; he held a service in the church there four or five times a year, *'not oftener…for want of a congregation'*.[2] Allerston with sixty and Ebberston with eighty families were both considerably bigger places than Levisham. We picture Wykes living in Levisham, travelling to Kirby Grindalythe, Allerston and Ebberston to carry out his commitments there, with help from Deason when he was not busy with his duties at Middleton, Cropton and Lockton.

There was no school in Levisham, but Wykes claimed to teach the village children and servants who were sent to him for instruction in *'the principals of the Christian Religion according to the doctrine of the Church of England'*.[3]

The Church acted as the guardian of morality, with a keen eye for fornication. At the end of his answers to Archbishop Herring,

[2] Herring   [3] ibid

Wykes noted: '*Fornication* — *C.D. bastard child. Excommunicated and denounced*'. There was a printed Form of Penance[4] prescribed, requiring the culprit to stand front of the pulpit, bare headed, bare legged, wrapped in a white sheet, repeating a formal confession in the presence of the congregation — a very public humiliation in an age when everyone was required to attend church.

The Wykes' income from their Levisham benefice came from an oxgang of arable land in the open fields, rights of grazing on the common, tithes on '*wool, lamb, corn, hay, calves, foals, bees, pigs, geese, ducks, chickens*' and a tithe of three shillings and four pence per year from the Mill. There were fees from marriages, (ten shillings with a license, two shillings with banns), churchings, (eight pence) and burials (two shillings).

Wykes senior died in 1752 aged seventy nine; does the absence of any entries in the Parish Registers for the last sixteen years of his life suggest a certain loss of efficiency? On his father's death, young Isaac was immediately ordained in York, the one non-graduate amongst the seventeen ordinands, and was instituted to the Levisham Rectory to which his mother Mary held the right of presentation — keeping it all in the family. He took over from his father as curate in Allerston and Ebberston, moving to live in Ebberston for the later years of his life. In the year of his ordination he married an Allerston girl, Hannah Baker; their one child Rachel married a Lockton farmer, Thomas Robinson. At the time of the Levisham Enclosure, 1770, Wykes was one of the two largest Levisham landowners, he and Robert Harding, gentleman, of Marishes each holding ninety-one acres. We have no way of knowing how the two Wykes divided their time between their clerical duties and their land management, but the gaps in the Parish Registers during both incumbencies suggest a certain slackness in parish administration. They may, perhaps, represent some of the deficiencies in the Anglican ministry which gave rise to the Methodist revival — deficiencies recognised by Canon Atkinson, writing towards the end of the nineteenth century about his predecessors in the moorland area around Danby.[5]

---

[4] Borthwick

[5] Atkinson p.15

In 1779, Wykes sold the Rectory to Robert Harding – the parsonage house, land, tithes, presentation to the living – and went to live in Ebberston while continuing to officiate as Levisham's Rector. It was Harding who nominated Wykes' successor, Robert Skelton.

Wykes and Skelton were both from families from the local area. There had been Skeltons with land in Levisham a century earlier; Skeltons in Sinnington and Middleton listed amongst Yorkshire families in the seventeenth century, the Middleton Skeltons sporting a coat of arms.[6] The Robert Skelton who came to Levisham as Rector in 1786 was the only son of a Middleton yeoman (described in the Parish Register record of his son's birth as 'labourer'), who had sufficient property to be able to refer in his will (1783) to '*…all my parcel of lands wheresoever situated …*', and to bequeath to his wife '*…one of my houses which she chooses…*'. Robert was the sole heir. By the time of his father's death, he had been ordained in Gloucester (why there – ?) and then returned to his home area to take up the Perpetual Curacy of Rosedale. Four years later, he was appointed to the Rectory of Levisham.

Levisham records during the early years of Skelton's time in Levisham provide more evidence of his acquisitions of land than his church affairs. His name keeps recurring in the register of Deeds; in 1788 he bought a tenanted farm, two more houses in 1793; in 1797, another farm and the purchase of fifteen acres of land in Newtondale. His biggest investment was to buy in 1792 the title to the Manor of Levisham along with '*that newly erected messuage*', Levisham Hall.

As we have noted earlier, the Manorial title had been acquired during the mid-eighteenth century by William Poad, a Levisham yeoman, who held it at the time of the Enclosure in 1770. On Poad's death, his son sold the property and title to the Manor to Anthony Oates Esq. of Pickering. The Deeds for this transaction refer to the site '*… wherein a Mansion House once stood…*'. By the time Skelton bought the property from Oates' executors, there was a '*newly erected messuage or Mansion House*' to move into with his wife Sarah and three children, Sarah, Robert and John. The old Parsonage House, described in a

---

[6] Dugdale's Visitation p.437

Terrier dated 1809 as *'very ancient, all built with stone and thatched'*, was let as a farm. By this time, Skelton had under his control three hundred acres in addition to the ninety or so acres of Glebe land within Levisham, as well as property in other parts of the district. The Register of Deeds records his property transactions in Middleton, Cropton, Aislaby, Hartoft, Wrelton, Gillamoor, Thornton, Malton, Pickering.[7] He had arrived as a landed gentleman.

He had expansionist plans for the church as well as for himself and his family. He aimed to modernise the old medieval Parish Church of St Mary. In 1801, the chancel was restored at the expense jointly of the Rector and the Parish, with a vault for the Skelton family within the altar rails. The following year, the rest of the church was completely rebuilt, leaving only the chancel arch from the original church. The ancient font, roughly carved with a cross and bishop's crozier was banished to a farmyard for use as a cattle trough. In the churchyard, Skelton built a stone stable near the gate for his own use.[8] His responsibility for the parish of Rosedale as well as Levisham necessitated a great deal of time on horseback.

In 1814, Robert Skelton junior was ordained and appointed curate to his father at a salary of sixty guineas a year (Wykes' curate had received twenty pounds a year in 1738). Perhaps the elder Skelton's health was failing; he died four years later, to be succeeded by his son who served as rector for the next fifty-nine years. Two Diocesan Returns from 1865 and 1868 give a picture of church life during his incumbency.[9] Like his father, he held the benefice of Rosedale and looked after both parishes without the help of a curate. Each Sunday, he conducted two services, one at Levisham, the other at Rosedale; alternately morning or afternoon, preaching a sermon at each service. The Sacrament was administered to an average of twelve communicants three or four times a year. His congregation at ordinary services averaged about fifty to eighty out of a total population of around a hundred and fifty, the size affected by the weather. Sometime around 1850, the Chapel of Ease in the village,

[7] Register of Deeds. NYCRO
[8] Terrier 1809
[9] Borthwick

which had been used for services in the winter, collapsed and Skelton was aggrieved that there was no help forthcoming towards its restoration. He wrote,

> 'The Church is in a valley and the road is dirty in stormy wet weather and the hill very steep to climb'...

and lamented:

> 'the old chapel (is) in <u>ruins</u> and wish to know by what means I am to obtain <u>funds</u> to rebuild it. I got Rosedale church rebuilt by subscription, and my own labours, and endeavours...and begged and collected and paid every Bill against it...but dare not undertake to rebuild Levisham old Chapel. The Parish is so small, and the inhabitants many of them poor.'[10]

By this time there was also a Primitive Methodist ('Ranter') chapel in Levisham offering an alternative for those not wanting to tackle the hill down into the valley. The neighbouring village of Lockton, with a tradition of religious dissent, (perhaps because as an outlying chapelry of the parish of Middleton it did not have its own resident clergyman) had a Methodist Society in 1797; by the mid-nineteenth century the village supported both a Wesleyan and a Primitive Methodist chapel.[11] There was a Primitive Methodist society in Levisham by 1842 when the Circuit Plan records a Sunday meeting every fortnight and a monthly Monday meeting. Their little chapel was built in 1859, two Levisham farmers, John Poad and Robert Stead, among the nine trustees.[12]

Skelton's seven daughters provided him with a supply of teachers for the Sunday School. By 1868, a widower, all his daughters married and gone except for one who kept house for him, he had to admit that the school was not so well run.

Robert Skelton II took over his father's role as landowner and Lord of the Manor as well as Rector. The 1848 Tithe Award shows him as owner of the Mill and four tenanted farms as well as a hundred and thirty acres he owned and managed himself, together with around a hundred acres of Glebe land. He rebuilt the old Parsonage House,[13]

---

[10] DiocesanReturns 1865& 1868:Borthwick

[11] Strong

[12] Register of Deeds NYCRO

[13] Terrier 1865

built a house near the station (Grove House)[14] and put up a Tower on the moor with a stable on the ground floor and an upstairs room with magnificent views over Newtondale. Like many country gentlemen, he took an interest in 'antiquities', and dug out some of the barrows on Levisham Moor. His name appears amongst those interested in the project for building a canal in Newtondale before the railway project superseded it.

In the mid-1850's, he got into financial difficulties for reasons that have not been discovered. He sold his Levisham properties, including the Hall and manorial title, retiring to live down at Grove House which had been bought by his son-in-law, Robert Hansell. A notice to his creditors was published in the local press;[15] amongst them were the Levisham Overseers of the Poor. A note in the Poor Book records that sums of money totalling £110.17.0 raised by sales of land '...*were placed in the care of the Revd Robert Skelton, the then Rector and Lord of the Manor of Levisham, who paid interest regularly up to about 1855 about which time his affairs passed into liquidation in Bankruptcy...*'.

The style of clerical life represented by the Wykes and Skelton Rectors disappeared with them. A Rector might, like J.E. Armstrong at the end of the nineteenth century, be a gentleman of means, (Armstrong built and lived in his own house, now called The Moorlands), but never again were they figures who attempted to combine the role of leading village landowner with pastor of the church. A more professional clergy had emerged.

---

[14] Whellan's Directory 1859

[15] Yorkshire Gazette June 25th 1856

Chapter 11: Enclosure and After
Farming 18th and 19th centuries

Green Cottage, built 1791: one of the post-Enclosure farmhouses in Levisham

CHRONOLOGY

1750-1815	Enclosure Movement at its height
1770	Levisham Enclosure
1836	Tithe Commutation Act
1848	Levisham Tithe Award

SOURCES

Documentary	On the ground
Enclosure Awards, maps	Field boundaries
Tithe Awards	Roads
Register of Deeds	Houses
Land Tax	
Marshall: Rural Economy of Yorkshire	
Tuke: General View of Agriculture of the North Riding	

Where a village or town had an open field system, there is likely to be an Enclosure Award from the late eighteenth or early nineteenth century detailing the manner in which the land was redistributed, probably accompanied by a map. An Enclosure Award gives a complete survey of the land and its ownership.

Another such comprehensive survey was carried out following the Tithe Commutation Act when, in order to translate the Tithe into a money payment, it was necessary to establish the acreage and value of all land. By the time of the Tithe maps and schedules there are census returns which along with Parish Registers help to fill out the picture of village society.

Yorkshire and Middlesex are the only two counties to have a Register of Deeds: this valuable record of all property transactions after 1763 in the NYCRO is useful in tracing the history of particular properties, and giving some sense of what was happening in the property market. Land Tax returns between 1781 and 1832 provide the names of owners and occupiers of land and their tax assessment.

Two contemporary writers on farming on North Yorkshire, William Marshall and John Tuke, exemplify contemporary attitudes to agricultural improvement: a rational approach drawing on scientific knowledge, a subject for investigation and innovation.

Background

The eighteenth century saw the start of a fundamental change in the economic base of English society. From being predominantly rural society, with most of the population living in villages and earning a living from the land, there was a shift towards urban centres and industry. By the time of the 1871 census, the majority of the population lived in towns and only 15% of the working population was engaged in agriculture. The scientific and technological knowledge used to develop new methods of industrial production was applied also to agriculture, which became more productive, more mechanised and more market orientated.

The enclosure of the open fields, where they still existed, was part of the modernisation process. Some enclosures were carried out by local agreement, some by Act of Parliament. Enclosure benefited the enterprising farmer with an interest in innovation, with some capital and an eye to greater profitability. The word that was used regularly as justification for the enclosure was 'improvement'. With enclosure, the whole appearance of the landscape changed from the large, unfenced fields cultivated in rotation, one lying fallow each year, to the patchwork of much smaller hedged, walled or fenced fields we are familiar with today.

Enclosure was generally to the advantage of the better off, and is credited with forcing off the land the smaller, less efficient men. It provides a landmark moment in the history of an agricultural community.

The years following this widespread enclosure movement were generally a time of prosperity, with new money invested, new agricultural methods introduced, productivity increased to meet demands of growing towns and of a nation at war with France. After the wars ended, agricultural fortunes fluctuated. A depression in the 1820's and 1830's was followed by the period of so-called 'high farming' of the mid-century which in the last quarter of the century was followed by another agricultural decline as a flood of imported grain from the newly opened-up plains of America was transported across the Atlantic in steam ships.

Levisham

On January 29th 1770, the 'owners and proprietors' of the farmland of Levisham headed by William Poad, Gentleman, Lord of the Manor, Robert Harding, William Harding, Ralph Greystock together with the Reverend Isaac Wykes, Rector and owner of the advowson and the Tythes, entered into a formal agreement to arrange for the enclosure of the open fields. The agreement recited that:

> '... there then were within the Township and Parish of Levisham ... three large fields called Limpseygate Field, Braygate Field and Little Field containing altogether about five hundred acres and which did lye open and unenclosed and the lands of the several proprietors therein greatly intermixed and dispersed so that in their then condition the same could not be improved...'.[1]

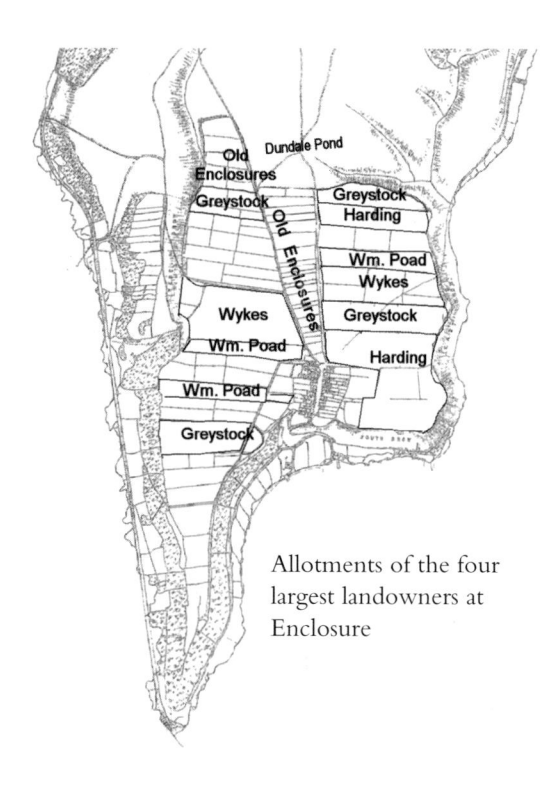

Allotments of the four largest landowners at Enclosure

---

[1] Levisham Enclosure Award: NYCRO

Four Commissioners were named *'with full power.... to cause a survey and admeasurement to be made...'* after which they were to reapportion the land, with *'indifference and impartiality'*, giving *'due and equal regard to convenience and advantage of all parties'*, and taking into account quality as well as quantity of land. Isaac Wykes was to receive one seventh of the total in lieu of Tithes, except for the Tithe of wool and lamb which he was to retain.

The Commissioners set to work: Robert Lythe, Mark Staines the younger, John Ffoord, Thomas Dodsworth. Mark Staines died before their work started, and was replaced by Robert King. They had *'many meetings'*, *'viewed all the fields well'* several times, assessing land quality as well as extent, *'maturely considered'* the requirement for access roads, drainage ditches, stiles, gates, bridges, and by October had arrived at their conclusions, *'the whole award being contained in Eight Skins of Parchment'*.

Of the four 'owners and proprietors' named in the preamble to the award, William Harding, does not appear again; the other three, Robert Harding, Greystock and Poad, together with the Rector, Isaac Wykes, held between them over sixty percent of the land. The rest was shared between sixteen people, two with very small holdings of less than an acre. The three largest allotments went to Isaac Wykes, Robert Harding (ninety-one acres each), and Ralph Greystock (eighty-seven acres). William Poad, Lord of the Manor, had only about half as much (forty-eight acres); already, it seems, newer men outstripping the long-established local figure. Neither Harding nor Greystock lived in Levisham – Harding is described as 'gentleman', of Marishes, Greystock 'yeoman' of Pickering. Six of the other land-owners lived elsewhere – Crosscliffe, Wilton, Goathland, Burniston, Lockton, Craike.[2]

The composition of the village had already been changing significantly during the previous century. A number of the 'core families' had disappeared; those remaining, such as Poad and Read, had moved lower down the land-owning league table. Greystock, who had

---

[2] The Enclosure Award only covers the land in the three open fields; there was an additional sixty three acres which had been enclosed previously – referred to as 'old enclosures'.

come to the village some forty-five years earlier and married into one of the 'core families' seems to have prospered.[3] His very stylish signature on a deed of 1736, a date when a number of the chief inhabitants were unable to sign their names and had to make their mark when witnessing official documents, suggests that he was a man of above the average ability and education. By that date, he had moved to Haghouse, Thornton and become a butcher. The old pattern of families subsisting on a holding of land built around a share of the common arable fields and passed down through the generations, was giving way to a more market-oriented approach to farming. In the middle years of the eighteenth century, land was coming to be seen as an investment. The Register of Deeds contains the names of people investing in Levisham land who had no other connection with the village: a Scarborough widow, a York plumber and glazier, a dealer in hardware from Kirkbymoorside, a clockmaker. The name of Robert Harding, along with the Rector, Isaac Wykes one of the two largest landowners in 1770, first appears amongst the Levisham entries in the Register of Deeds during the 1760s. He never lived in the village, but he and his heirs were to own considerable land in Levisham for the next two centuries. Enclosure was not so much the beginning of a process of change as the recognition and endorsement of change that was already under way.

In the decade following enclosure, the progress of this accelerating process of change can be followed in the Register of deeds and the Parish registers. William Poad died in 1771; the next year his son John sold his property including the title to the manor to a Pickering gentleman, Anthony Oates. Harding continued to acquire property in Levisham, including the tithes and advowson when Wykes left to spend his last years in Ebberston. New people moved into the village: a dozen new names in the marriage and baptism registers, suggest the arrival of young families. Some can be recognised as belonging to the 'yeoman' class, their names figuring in the lists of Parish officers or in the Deeds register. Others were 'labourers', whose names recur later in the Poor Book.

[3] see chapter 9: Family Life

Two contemporary writers on the agriculture of the area, William Marshall and John Tuke, both describe the typical farming people they met on their travels round the North Riding. Tuke noted that the farms in the eastern Moorlands were small, the farming people *'generally sober, industrious and orderly'*, and that *'most of the younger part of them have enjoyed a proper education'*. On the other hand, he recognised certain limitations. *'It is observable'* he said, *'that in those families that have succeeded from generation to generation in the same farm, the strongest attachment to old customs prevails; such have the most confined ideas…'*. Marshall saw the farmers as people happy in their independent character, but on the whole not interested in improvement or increased productivity. These observations may help to explain what was happening in Levisham during the late eighteenth century, the old-established farmers finding it hard to adapt to changes, new men coming in who had less *'confined ideas'*.

Anyone visiting Levisham today passes along lanes wide enough to drive through, bounded by stone walls and overlooking fields divided by either walls or hedges. The roads, the walls, the hedges were all prescribed in the Enclosure Award which specified precisely the width of the roads and who was responsible for constructing *'at his own expense'* a *'good ditch'* here, a fence there. Ralph Graystock, for example, was to fence his fields in Limpseygate Field, one of fifteen acres, one twenty eight acres; along the south side of the latter field he was to *'plant…with Quickwood and fence such Quickwood with good and sufficient posts and rails'*. There is a hedge there today; perhaps Graystock's hedge? The nurserymen selling Quickset Thorns at around 5s to 12s 6d per thousand[4] must have been doing a brisk trade during this period of Enclosure, while the quarries near the village would have been kept busy providing the stone for the field walls and the new house building that was undertaken.

The increased number of entries in the Register of Deeds relating to land in Levisham in the years after Enclosure suggests a buoyant property market.

---

[4] Catalogue Backhouse Nursery, York 1821. York Library.

It was a time when there was money for new house building. No traces survive of the fabric of any Levisham houses before the eighteenth century, but a number of the present village houses, while substantially altered, originally date from the post-Enclosure period. Most appear to have been built as traditional stone longhouses: a style of farm house one room deep, living quarters at one end, byre at the other. The present Green Cottage was such a house, dated 1791 on the byre end.[5] Low Grange farm buildings can be dated from the 1802 on the end of one barn. Levisham Hall dates from this time, a double-fronted house put up by Oates, probably a bit of speculative building as he never appears to have lived there. When Robert Skelton bought the house in 1792 it was described in the deeds as *'that newly erected Mansion House…'*.[6] Meanwhile, the former Manor House was left to fall into ruins.

Another phase of building came later in the nineteenth century when farming was again doing well. The houses of this time were likely to be larger and built on a square plan: one, Grange Farm, has the date 1860, on the lintel over the front door. The two Skeltons. father and son, were enthusiastic builders. During their time, the Hall was enlarged, the old Rectory rebuilt, the house called Homestead House, (now Newton House Farm) rebuilt.[7] Later, after the arrival of the railway, Skelton built a house down in Newtondale near the station (now Grove House), to which he retired after selling the Hall in 1856.[8] Miles Close, son-in-law of the elder Skelton, built the present Glebe Farm.

Between these two periods of farming prosperity came the down turn during the post-war years, in the 1820's and 1830's. Robert Merry of Lockton was one of those called to give evidence to the Select Committee on Agriculture of the House of Commons in 1833. He had inherited a farm of around three hundred acres in Lockton, but also managed various properties in the area, and worked as a land surveyor and valuer, so had the opportunity to get an all-round view of the agricultural scene in the North Riding. In his evidence, he

---

[5] Mercer p.224

[6] NYCRO Register of Deeds CJ 43 75

[7] Deed IH 418 633

[8] Deed

paints a picture of twenty years of falling prices for farm produce resulting in farmers falling into debt, labourers being laid off, landowners unable to find tenants for their farms. He said: *'There is less money stirring'*; labourers' wages had fallen from 3s 6d a day to about 2s. With less to spend on farm upkeep, hedges were *'worse dressed up'*, land drainage was neglected, there was less lime burned to fertilise the land, less stock kept. People were even reluctant to call the doctor when they were ill because they could not afford the bill. Those engaged in farming discovered that Enclosure had not brought in a golden age to last for ever.

The map that accompanied the Enclosure Award has not survived, but has been reconstructed from the detailed written description of the allocations.[9] The map that emerges, its field boundaries and roads, was almost unchanged at the time of the Tithe map in 1848, was still the same at the 1910 Valuation, and is not much altered today.

The work of the Enclosure commissioners laid down the pattern of the agricultural landscape for years to come. Roads and lanes, field boundaries – walls or hedges – are today much as were determined then, but the pattern by which farming was financed and organised soon showed signs of changes which can be read from the Land Tax returns.[10]

Land Tax was assessed for a township as a whole, a little over twenty pounds in the case of Levisham. This sum was then divided proportionately amongst the land-owners. The lists name first the owner, then the occupier (who was liable for the payment) followed by the amount due. In 1781 the Levisham assessment ranged from the highest payer:-

Owner	Occupier	£	s	d
Mr Harding	Richard Woodcock			
	John Green	3	14	7

to the lowest:-

Elizabeth Walmsley	Philip Burnet		1	6

[9] Transcription of Enclosure Award and reconstructed map by F.T. Lea, in Levisham Village Archives

[10] NYCRO

There were thirty owners, seven with a tax rating of over one pound. For some years the number of owners increased to a peak of thirty-seven in 1788, the increase amongst the lower rated: perhaps people seizing an opportunity to come in on an agricultural boom by buying a small plot of land. The higher rated were the owners of the established farms, and their number remained constant throughout the nineteenth century. There was, however, a shift in the balance between owner-occupiers and tenants. A majority of owner-occupiers in 1793 had changed by the end of the century to a majority of tenants. This was followed by a further change as the number of owners decreased until in 1848, at the time of the Tithe Award, three owners, Robert Skelton (Rector and Lord of the Manor), Henry Harding (descendent of the Harding of the Enclosure) and James Dixon, (who had come to the village during the 1780's) owned between them more than half of the cultivated land of Levisham. The optimistic expansion that came in the aftermath of Enclosure had not lasted. The survivors seem to be those with the means to buy up more land. But Robert Skelton who in 1848 occupied Levisham Hall and the hundred or so acres that went with it, who also owned the Mill and four tenanted farms, got into financial difficulties and was forced to sell out in 1856. James Dixon, at Lowstead farm in 1848, was in the 1851 census no longer owning the farm but described as 'agricultural labourer'. Only the Hardings with a financial base elsewhere continued to own a substantial amount of Levisham land throughout the century.

The next fixed point at which it is possible to get a complete view of the agricultural scent is the 1910 Valuation, (carried out to assess the value of land in preparation for the levying of a tax which was never implemented).[11] It shows eight working farms together with the mill, ranging in size from two hundred and thirty acres to thirty four acres, all run by tenant farmers. The Harding Trustees were the owners of the largest amounts of agricultural land, the interests of the owner of the Hall no longer in farming but the sporting potential of the Moor.

---

[11] Schedule and map in PRO; schedule only NYCRO.

Chapter 12: Village School

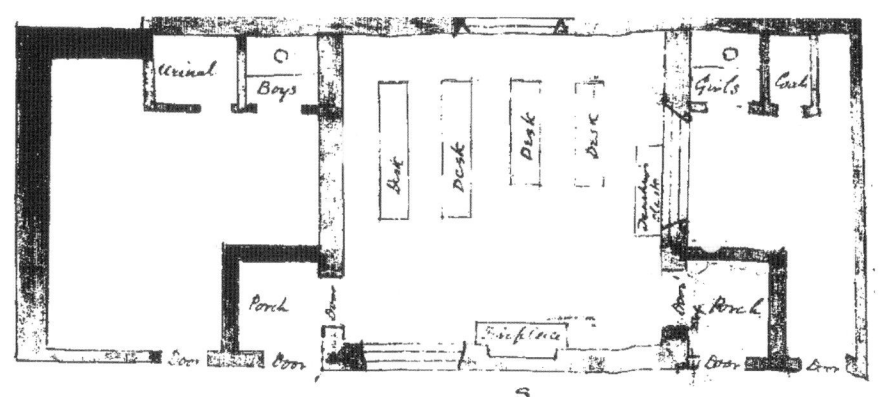

Plan of Levisham School building
*from the nineteenth century -
the building, now a house, still
identifiable by its belfry.*
© *Crown Copyright*

CHRONOLOGY

National		Local	
		1793	Endowment to provide school in Levisham
1833	1st Government grants to voluntary Societies for education of the poor		
1846	Pupil Teacher system; certificates for teachers		
1870	Forster's Education Act: School Boards	1877	Levisham School Board
1880	Compulsory education		
1891	Free elementary education		
		1939	Levisham school closed

SOURCES

Herring's Visitation	YAS Record Series
Minutes of Committee of Council for Education	Government papers
School Log Books (none for Levisham)	NYCRO
Levisham Vestry Minutes	NYCRO
Correspondence with Department of Education	PRO

The answers to the question about parish schools in Herring's Visitation of 1743 provide a picture of educational provision in mid-eighteenth century villages.

Once the Government became involved in education early in the next century through provision of funding for schools provided by the voluntary (church-based) societies, an Inspectorate was established to ensure that public money was being properly used. The Inspectors' reports to the Committee of Council for Education give a picture of the state of schools in the country as a whole. Information about individual schools can be gained from the Log Books that Head Teachers were required to keep – when these have survived. (There is one for Lockton, none for Levisham.) Information about the school of a particular village may come from references in Directories, Census Returns ('scholar' by the name of a child attending school), and other local records which may refer to a school teacher or school building.

Background

The dearth of village schools before the late eighteenth century would not have been felt as a serious deprivation. Literacy was useful for certain occupations, but was not necessary for those whose jobs did not bring them into touch with books or the need to engage in written calculations of some sort. It was no more a universal requirement than was computer literacy a few years ago.

In 1743, one of the questions asked in Archbishop Herring's Visitation was whether there was a school in the parish. Of the forty one parishes that made up the Ryedale Deanery, twenty three – over half – had no school. There were two boys' Grammar schools , one at Old Malton endowed by Archbishop Holgate with thirty to forty boys on its roll, one at Thornton Dale endowed by Lady Lumley, *'wherein a great number of Gentlemen's sons are educated as well as children of the town'*. Five villages had schools described as 'private' or 'petty' or 'English' schools – 'petty' meaning small, a handful of children in the teacher's living room; 'English' in that they were not, like Grammar schools, teaching Latin, just basic literacy. They were privately run by someone trying to make or supplement an income from them, for example a weaver in Goathland, 'an old man' in Sinnington. Ten villages had schools provided by a small local charitable endowment of a few pounds to pay a schoolmaster to teach a few poor children. In Appleton le Street, an endowment provided a salary of £4.10s per year for a schoolmaster, and the Trustees had acquired a piece of ground on which they intended putting up a school building. Cropton had a charity school endowed with £5 or £6 to pay for the instruction of six poor scholars. In Nunnington, as well as £7 a year for the education of eight poor children there was a dwelling house for the schoolmaster, while in Normanby the parishioners had put up a school building and a local benefactor, Mrs Boynton, endowed it with £5 per year.

There was as yet no such thing as a teaching profession. Anyone could set up a school, in whatever premises were available: no training needed, no qualifications asked for. The schoolmaster in Appleton le Street had recently been dismissed at the time of the Herring Visitation for being *'troublesome'*; the teacher at Salton was *'a poor man's son'* who was a cripple. Whether or not a parish had a school, the incumbent was expected to provide religious teaching based on the Church of England catechism to local children and servants.

Changes in society produced new educational needs. Some elementary schooling became necessary to transmit the skills needed in a more technical age. There was another motive for providing schools for the poor: with revolutionary mobs striking terror across the Channel and evident unrest in both agricultural and industrial areas of England, education was seen as a possible tool for inculcating attitudes of deference, of respect for authority. There was a counter argument in the debate: might not education be a dangerous means of raising aspirations and fomenting discontent amongst the lower orders?

The provision of schools for the poor was originally an object for private charity, then for voluntary societies associated with the churches, and finally for the state. Government involvement in the form of grant-aid to the voluntary societies started in 1833, at a time when it was estimated that only 9% of the population attended school. Only after the 1870 Education Act was there anything approaching a national system of elementary education, when elected School Boards were empowered to provide rate-aided schools for all.

Once the Government had a financial stake in education through its grant aid, it had an interest in efficiency and recruited a team of Inspectors whose reports to the Committee of Council for Education give a picture of the schools they visited, – the buildings, teachers, pupils, curriculum. They were an enlightened band of educational pioneers (drawn mainly from the ranks of Anglican clergymen, but with the poet Matthew Arnold amongst their number), who saw education as a road to personal and social betterment. '*A great object of education*', wrote one, '*is to make them think…*',[1] but they recognised that it was an uphill task, and that these schools were starting from a very low base.

---

[1] Rev.F.Watkins 1845

Levisham

In 1793, John Poad, gentleman, of Lockton died, leaving in his will a bequest of £11 a year chargeable on a property he owned in Normanby, to the Churchwardens and Overseers of the Poor of Levisham *'towards the expenses of keeping a school in Levisham and teaching so many of the poor children belonging to the …Townships of Lockton and Levisham as the Churchwardens and Overseers of the Poor of Levisham shall see fit so there be an equal number from both Townships…'*

The following year, the first Schoolmaster, Mr. John Ellis, was appointed, and the Trustees met in the Chapel of Ease (*'the School House being not yet erected'*) to select the first free scholars: five from each village – Ann and Eleanor Gibb, John and James Ward and John Harlan from Levisham, William and James Allanson, Grace Atkinson, Abel and Esther Simpson from Lockton. Each year thereafter the Minutes of the annual Vestry Meeting record that after a session in the Chapel electing the Parish officers for the year, the meeting adjourned to the School for the nomination of the free scholars. The Minutes list names, but tell us nothing about the process of selection. Poad's will did not specify the number of beneficiaries, only that there was to be an equal number from Levisham and Lockton. From 1817 onwards, the number was always six from each village, but before that the number varied, some years only two, in other years, three. Was there little demand for these free school places? Was there a feeling amongst families struggling to make ends meet that their children's time could be more usefully spent than sitting on a school bench? We have nothing to indicate how the innovation of a village school was received.

From 1817 onwards, there was always the full complement of six Levisham free scholars. The names Jackson, Stockill, Morley, Wallis, Dixon keep recurring, all names of families known from other sources to be recipients of parish relief. However, there are some names that give point to the response made by the schoolmaster in a survey by the Committee of Council of Education that *'several farmers' children who have no claim are entered among the poor, the endowment being totally for poor children…'*.[2] The Tates (on the list between 1832 and 1839) were

---

[2] Parliamentary Papers 1835. Abstract of answers and returns on State of Education in England and Wales

children of the miller, the Colliers, children of a farmer; there were also Lightowlers, children of the schoolmaster who made the complaint! Most of the children continued on the list for six or seven years. If even some of these were children who would not otherwise have had any schooling, then John Poad's bequest performed a most valuable service for several generations.

For the first thirty-five years, there was always a preponderance of boys amongst the free scholars; then the balance changes with a more equal gender distribution – even, in some years, a majority of girls.

The school building was put up around 1799.[3] A Terrier of 1809 refers to the *'schoolhouse, built by public subscription...'*; according to White's Directory (1840), the school *'has space for another four rooms which might be occupied by the master, but they have never been finished.'* Ten years later, another directory entry speaks of the 'dilapidated' school building. What this early school building was like, we do not know. On Monday, December 19th 1869, the school was burned down and left in ruins, according to a hand-written note-book of Robert Skelton. For the time being, the school was conducted in the Hall (referred to as the Manor House), at that time standing empty; it was still being used as a schoolroom at the time of the 1871 Census. The rebuilding of the school was discussed in a letter from Joseph Ward, Esq. of Levisham to the Department of Education in 1875, but does not appear to have gone ahead until 1877 by which time the educational scene had changed.

Early in the nineteenth century, Henry Lightowler from Scagglethorpe was appointed school teacher at Levisham. The first appearance of his name in village records is his marriage in 1816 to Rachel Stead, daughter of a Levisham farmer. He continued at his post until compelled to resign through ill health in 1868, when he must have been in his mid-seventies. During his career, teaching in a small village school was not a full-time occupation. The £11 from the Poad bequest, plus whatever small fees (usually a penny a week) were paid by scholars, would not have made up a living wage for a man with a

---

[3] according to Whellan's Directory 1851

family of seven children. At one time, Lightowler was landlord of the Horseshoe Inn; later, he was able to buy some land and described himself as 'farmer'; in the 1861 Census, he is entered as 'Schoolmaster and Parish Clerk', in Kelly's Directory 1872 as 'shopkeeper'.

While we can discover something about the circumstances of his family life and involvement in village affairs from parish records, his work as schoolmaster remains hidden. We can pick up a general impression of schools at this time from the reports on the schools in his area by the Rev. Frederick Watkins, Inspector of Schools for the north, an area stretching from Sheffield to Berwick-on-Tweed, from Flamborough Head to St Bees. Although Levisham school did not receive a Government grant so was not subject to inspection, similar schools in the area were visited: Kirby Misperton, for example: *'room in bad repair...';* Yedingham: *'a poor building...';* Allerston, where a young widow kept a school for girls *'at her fireside...'* where most time was spent on needlework and a little arithmetic. Watkins noted the almost total lack of any training amongst the teachers he met; his comment on one, *'...anxious to do his best, but has not at present much understanding of the art of teaching...'* could have been applied to many.

During the year 1843-4, Watkins visited a hundred and sixty two schools. As he travelled around his area, he discovered *'a rude and hardy race, (inhabiting) wide tracts of moorland...'*. The average age of leaving school was twelve, the average duration of schooling, two years. He encountered children going barefoot to school, using for their lessons books of 'inferior quality', sometimes writing in copy books made by parents or teacher from thin, spongy paper with brown paper covers. The teaching was all by rote, learning set answers to a series of questions with no requirement to understand what they were learning. He quoted an example:

What is the earth on which we live?

A sphere

Is it a perfect sphere?

No, an oblate spheroid.

Knowledge, he said, *'comes by rote and departs the same way...'*. He commented on parental attitudes, especially in agricultural districts where they doubted the direct usefulness of what the schools were teaching for later life. '*We wants a bit of reading and writing and summing but na'at else*'. He concluded that there was little hope of benefit to the children '*until they are taught more simply and livingly*'. Would this, we wonder, have been what Levisham school was like? Two school exercise books from the years 1864 and 1866 belonging to George Dixon, a Levisham boy attending Lockton school, have been preserved by his family. In his arithmetic book, the eleven-year-old worked on simple interest – 'if a gentleman buys a farm for £3320, how should he sell it to pay him 5 per cent?' and calculated the value of stocks and shares. Two years later, in his immaculate copperplate handwriting he was doing more advance arithmetical calculations, learning long division, copying out the rules for finding the square and cube roots of numbers, copying verses with a distinctly moral tone. This is not the mindless rote learning of obscure concepts that Watkins complained of, but is typical of educational practice of the time in laying on neatness rather than originality, memorising of rules rather than comprehension.

At least we know that practically all Levisham children were enrolled at school. In the 1851 Census, seventeen of the twenty children between the ages of five and twelve are recorded as 'scholars'. One twelve year old girl, two eleven year olds, a boy and a girl, have no occupation by their names; they could have been scholars who had recently left and had not yet found employment. This does not tell us anything about attendance rates, which judging from the Log Books of other schools were likely to have fluctuated according to weather, sickness (epidemics of illnesses like measles), and the seasonal requirements of farm work.

When Lightowler retired, Skelton's son (another Robert) took over the school; '*my son Robert Skelton commenced teaching the school children in the Manor House…*' his father wrote in his notebook (December 19th 1869), and in the 1871 Census Robert junior's occupation was given as 'schoolmaster'. He had been admitted to St Catherine's College, Cambridge in 1849, but apparently never took a degree.

The arrival of a new Rector, William Berry, in 1877 brought fresh vigour and vision into the running of the school. The new school building was at last going ahead, ready for opening in January 1877 when it was hoped the walls would have dried out. An undated plan probably comes from this time.[4]

Often, clergymen favoured denominational schools keeping education safely under their influence: Berry did not. He saw the way forward as changing the status of the school to a Board school, transferring its management from the Trustees (Rector and Churchwardens) to a School Board elected by the ratepayers, and thereby bringing it more directly into the state system, eligible for grants and under government inspection.

He prepared the ground in correspondence with the Education Department, seeking clarification about the regulations concerning grants. A debate went on in the village as to whether the school should apply to be examined so that it could qualify for a grant as 'efficient'; would it be entitled to a higher grant if a certificated teacher were employed? There were difficulties. The village was embroiled in some other controversial matter which meant it was not a favourable time for focussing minds and getting agreement on a new plan for the school. Berry himself was clearly keen to get things moving – '...*I am immensely anxious to have a thoroughly efficient (school)*'. He was planning to run a night school for the older village boys to make up as much as he could for what he saw as their '*former want of education*'. He must have been an effective campaigner as in November 1877 a meeting of the ratepayers of the parish agreed to the formation of a School Board which would rent the recently rebuilt schoolhouse from the Trustees for a nominal sum.

Berry set about raising the money still owing on the buildings so that the school could start again free of debt. He sought reassurance from the Department about problems that could arise for very small communities in meeting the salary of a teacher, £3 per head per child. There was a little niggling problem of the Poad bequest, the £11 to pay for twelve children, six from each village, at the school at Levisham. The schools in Lockton and Levisham were by this time both Board Schools; from 1880 schooling was compulsory, but until

[4] PRO

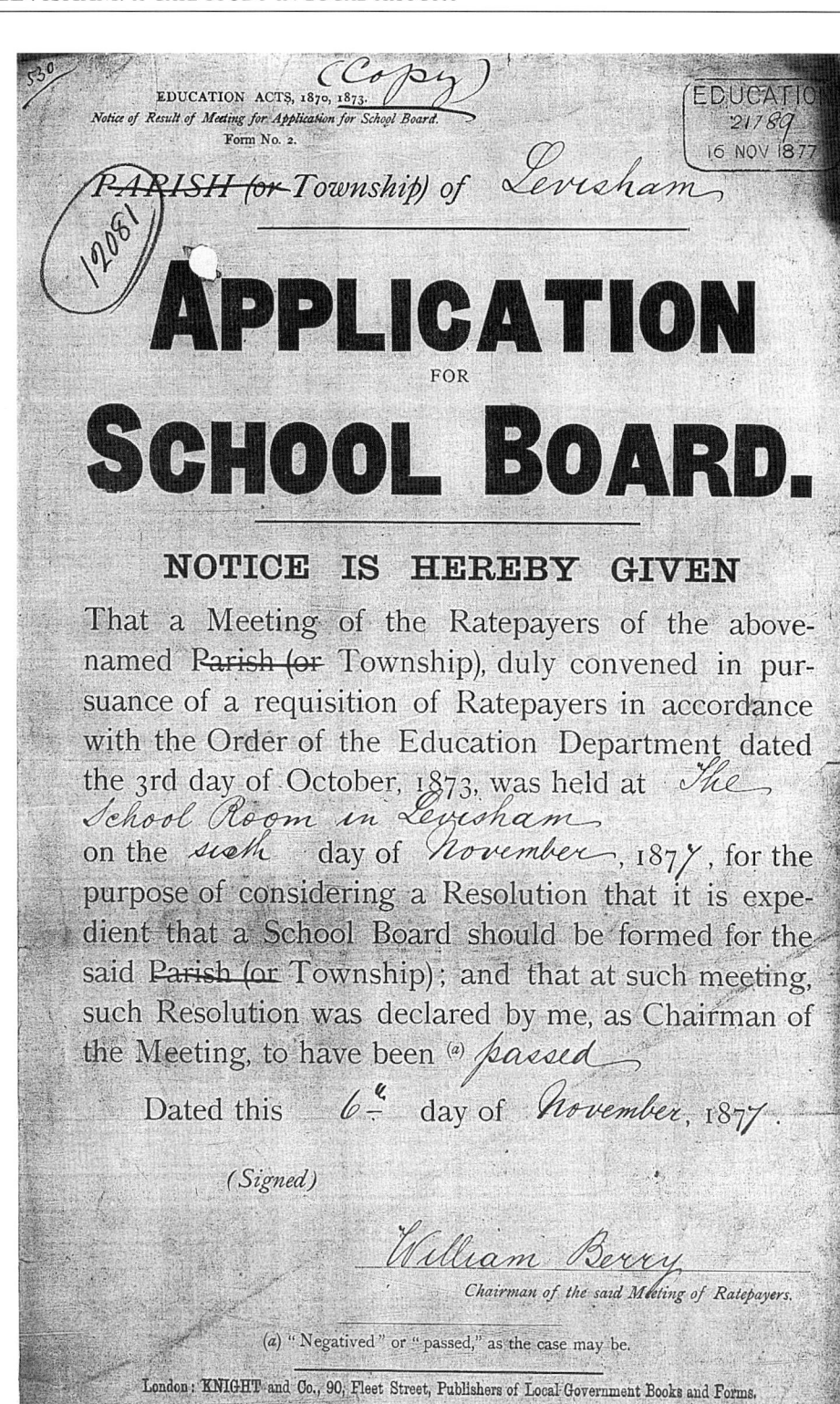

EDUCATION ACTS, 1870, 1873. (Copy)
Notice of Result of Meeting for Application for School Board.
Form No. 2.

EDUCATION
21789
16 NOV 1877

12081

~~PARISH (or~~ Township) of Levisham

APPLICATION
FOR
SCHOOL BOARD.

NOTICE IS HEREBY GIVEN

That a Meeting of the Ratepayers of the above-named ~~Parish (or~~ Township), duly convened in pursuance of a requisition of Ratepayers in accordance with the Order of the Education Department dated the 3rd day of October, 1873, was held at *The School Room in Levisham* on the *sixth* day of *November*, 1877, for the purpose of considering a Resolution that it is expedient that a School Board should be formed for the said ~~Parish (or~~ Township); and that at such meeting, such Resolution was declared by me, as Chairman of the Meeting, to have been (a) *passed*

Dated this 6th day of *November*, 1877.

(Signed)

William Berry
Chairman of the said Meeting of Ratepayers.

(a) "Negatived" or "passed," as the case may be.

London: KNIGHT and Co., 90, Fleet Street, Publishers of Local Government Books and Forms.

1891 it was not free so the Poad money still counted for something. The grievance of the Lockton School Board was that it all went to the Levisham school, the Lockton beneficiaries having to walk the steep mile down and up to Levisham: could the Lockton Board not have the £5.10, half the endowment? Such a question was beyond the scope of the Department of Education and had to be referred to the Charity Commissioners (whose reply has not been discovered).

After this flurry of activity instigated by William Berry, the school settled down, but with an ever-decreasing number on its rolls. At the end of the century, there were only sixteen on its register although it had room for forty-five pupils. Such a small school had difficulty in attracting and keeping teachers. A favourable Inspector's report in 1914 (*'the children show much interest and intelligence in their work...'*) was followed four years later by a note that the school had been unable to get a qualified teacher ...should the apparently satisfactory but unqualified Miss Magee be approved...?

In the years between the wars, the school continued with about a dozen pupils, but was finally closed in 1939. The final Inspector's report spoke of a school run on sensible lines, providing sound training in a classroom bright with flowers and pictures. Its closure marked the end of an era.

Commission

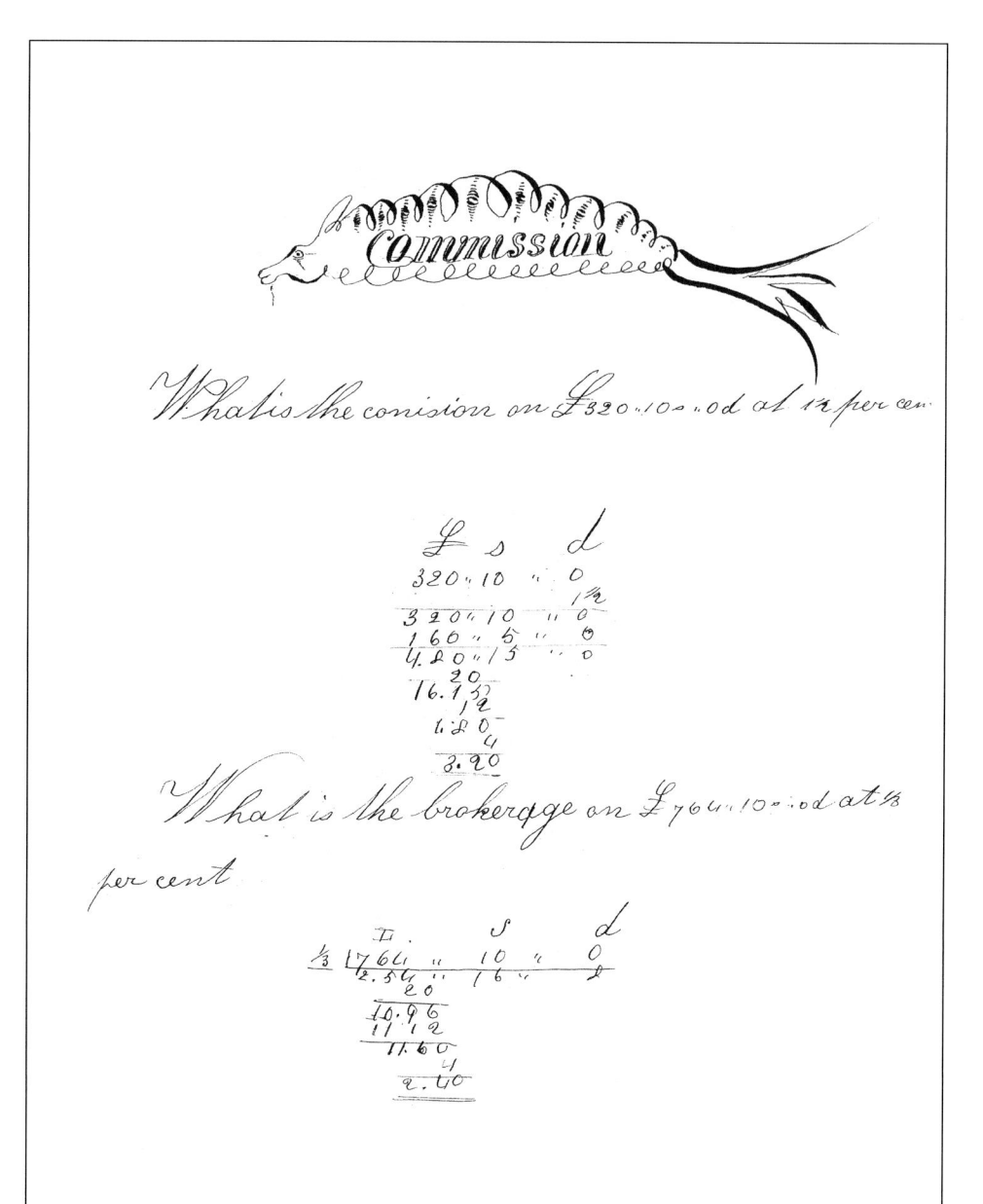

What is the conision on £320..10-..0d at 1½ per cent

```
        £     s    d
      320..10 ..  0
                      1½
      320..10 ..  0
      160.. 5  .. 0
      4.20..15 .. 0
           20
      16.1½
           ½
       £.8.0
           4
       3.20
```

What is the brokerage on £764..10-..0d at ⅓ per cent

```
         £      s     d
    ⅓  764 ..  10 ..  0
       2.54 .. 16 ..  8
            20
       10.96
       11  ½
       11.60
           4
       2.40
```

Page from George Dixon's School Book   Courtesy Olive Dixon

Chapter 13:
On the Breadline
Rural poverty in the 19thC

The type of ship in which emigrant families made the 2-month voyage from Whitby to Canada

CHRONOLOGY

1795	Speenhamland system
1793-1815	Revolutionary and Napoleonic Wars
1815	Corn Laws
1830's-1840's	Widespread rural discontent: pressure for repeal of Corn Laws. Emigration.
1834	Poor Law Amendment Act: workhouses

SOURCES

Document	Location
Parliamentary Papers	PRO; University Libraries
Levisham Poor Book	NYCRO
Correspondence between local Boards of Guardians and Poor Law Commissioners	PRO MH 12/14575, 12/14577
Local Newspapers: Yorkshire Gazette, Malton Mercury	Malton Library

The word 'pauper' in Census returns provides a starting point for recognising the number of people in a community unable to provide for themselves.

Any parish records relating to the Overseers of the Poor will be found in the County Record Office.

The Poor Law Amendment Act was overseen by Poor Law Commissioners, with Inspectors who monitored the work of the Unions. Correspondence between local Boards of Guardians and the Commissioners is in the PRO.

Background

The social problems relating to poverty took on new dimensions in England in the early nineteenth century, so much so that the Tudor Poor Law system of making the parish responsible for the poor within its boundaries was no longer adequate. The problems were most acute in the unplanned sprawl of industrial towns and cities, but rural areas were affected too with a larger class of wage-earning labourers liable to fall into poverty when harvests were poor, food dear or wages low. A system was devised of subsidising wages from the rates. First used in the Berkshire village of Speenhamland, it was adopted in other areas, where magistrates worked out tables to calculate the weekly payment allowable, based on the price of flour and the size of the family. The intention was humanitarian, but the effect was to discourage the payment of adequate wages.

During the Napoleonic Wars agriculture flourished; with a blockade preventing foreign imports, home-produced food was in huge demand. When the war ended the situation changed dramatically; imported food flooded in not only from Europe, but also for the first time from America, competing with home produce. The government's remedy: Corn Laws, imposing a duty on foreign corn to protect English farmers. The result was a rise in food prices, which helped farmers and landowners, but hurt both rural and urban wage-earners. Adding to the fears of agricultural workers was the introduction of mechanisation into farming. There was a violent reaction to the perceived threat to jobs posed by the introduction of threshing machines in the so-called 'Swing' riots of 1830, centred on East Anglia. In Dorset, agricultural labourers who attempted to strengthen their hand by forming a Union came up against the full force of the law and were sentence to deportation to the penal colony of Australia – the 'Tolpuddle Martyrs'.

One solution for those struggling to survive in both agricultural and industrial England was emigration. Three developing areas, the United States, Canada and Australia, were all competing to attract immigrants whose labour would help open up new territories. Societies were founded to promote emigration, and parishes were encouraged to help families ready to take up this option – in the year 1841, 1,058 emigrants were assisted by the poor rates. There is evidence from government papers, from parish records, from personal diaries and letters about this migration to the wide open spaces of America and Australia from an England where population growth was outstripping the demand for labour. Britain was perceived as having 'redundant' population, likely to provoke civil disorder and all manner of social ills.[1] In giving evidence to the Select Committee on

---

[1] Correspondence with Colonial Office.

Agriculture in 1833, Robert Merry of Lockton said *'there is not a township and hardly a family but what have some of their inhabitants and some of their relations gone to America, both labourers and farmers...'*.[2] The diary of the schoolmaster and parish clerk of the village of South Cave in the East Riding, Robert Sharp makes frequent reference to families from his parish choosing to emigrate.[3] He noted in his diary on January 25th 1830 that *'the emigration fever is pretty high here at present'*. He followed the fortunes of one family who sold up and took a passage on the Wilberforce, sailing from Hull to Quebec. They had a rough eight week voyage, but later in the year were able to write home about getting work for good wages which they hoped would make it possible to purchase *'a snug farm'*. Sharp was involved in parish meetings to consider requests for parish aid from prospective emigrants. One man with a family of three children was expecting to pay eight pounds ten shillings for passage money, and needed victuals for an estimated six week voyage. He was given the sixteen pounds he asked for, but the following year the parish turned down a request for fifteen pounds to enable a wife and children to join her husband in America. Similar discussions must have gone on in parish meetings up and down the country.

The most radical attempt to deal with the problem of poverty was the 1834 Poor Law Amendment Act by which parishes were grouped into Poor Law Unions under an elected Board of Guardians. In future, it was envisaged that poor relief would be given within the walls of the Union workhouse under strict, regimented conditions that would be a deterrent to all but the desperate. Workhouses were to remain dreaded places of last resort until their abolition with the advent of the Welfare State.

Levisham

There were various resources for relieving the poor in Levisham. The Overseers of the Poor were responsible for the annual collection and distribution of a rate known as the 'Poor Cess'. They also received

---

[2] Parliamentary Papers: Select Committee on Agriculture 1833

[3] Crowther p.244, 252

the income from a piece of land in Newtondale known locally as Charity Wood, and one pound a year payable at Whitsuntide *'out of a certain farm in the Parish of Glaisdale'*. They had at their disposal two cottages each with a piece of garden adjoining,[4] and there was the free education provided for six poor children of the parish from the will of John Poad.[5] The Charity Wood money appears to have been handled by the Rector, and between 1826 and 1833 the Pauper Book shows the receipt by the Overseers of a sum of around four pounds each Christmas from the Rev. Robert Skelton which was distributed to either eleven or twelve poor families.

The Levisham Pauper Book kept by the Overseers of the Poor opens with their accounts for the year 1828-9. In that year the rate, assessed at six pence in the pound, was collected by Overseer John Watson in two half-yearly instalments totalling twenty-seven pounds, five shillings. There were twenty-one ratepayers, five liable for payments of over one pound, the smallest a payment of six pence. The accounts were signed by three of the ratepayers and presented at the Quarter Sessions where they were accepted and countersigned by two magistrates, Henry Duncomb and Thomas Mitchelson. The cost of the trip, *'Book Laying Warrant and Journey: 7s'* figures in the list of disbursements.

In that year there were seven recipients of different forms of help. Two whose names occur regularly for several years are Edward Stockill and Margaret Gibb. The Parish Registers record the marriage of an Edward Stockill, 'servant', in 1777, and the marriage of David Gibb to his wife Margaret in 1779: here, it appears, were an agricultural labourer and an agricultural labourer's aged widow, long time residents in the village for whom the parish accepted responsibility in their old age. Each received a weekly allowance, four shillings a week to Stockill, two shillings to Margaret Gibb who also had her rent paid, fifteen shillings for a half year, and occasional house maintenance – a shilling for a new door lock, two pounds eight shillings for re-thatching. Both also received payments for *'leading turf*

---

[4] gardens now rented out as allotments by the Common Rights Committee

[5] see chapter Village School

from the High Moor': employment offered by the Parish to paupers at rates ranging from two shillings to three and sixpence a load. They were bringing down to the village loads of turf, which was the basic fuel until coal was brought in by the railway along Newtondale. The Overseers supplied turf to heat the school, one load a year, and looked after repairs to the school building.

Two others who received regular payments for 'leading turf' were Priscilla Jackson and John Morley, some time occupants of the two cottages owned by the Overseers; Jackson and Morley rented the gardens adjoining the cottages, so would have the means to help to feed their families. Priscilla was descended from a family that can be traced back in Levisham registers and wills to the mid-seventeenth century. She was born in 1768, daughter of Ammon Adamson whose name appears as one of the 'chief inhabitants' on Church Terriers. She married John Jackson of Lastingham in 1792. The baptism of their seven children and the burial of four of them at Levisham between 1792 and 1808 suggests that this was where their married life was spent – her husband was probably the John Jackson, yeoman whose name appears in property transactions in the Register of Deeds in 1792. There is no record of his death in the Levisham registers, but by 1828 when the Overseers accounts start she appears to be a widow. At the time of the 1841 Census, she was described as 'pauper', living with her daughter, a son James who was an agricultural labourer, a grandson and a six-year-old pauper child, Martha Young – of whom more later. Ten years later at the next Census she was still the head of her household, aged 82, daughter Mary and son John still living with her plus two grandsons. This time she is described as *'formerly dressmaker'*. From these scattered entries in different records we can discern the outline of a hard life, going down in the world, struggling by various means and with help from the parish to keep her household together. She and Margaret Gibb must have been tough characters, both still 'leading turves' when well into their eighties.

John Morley, an agricultural labourer, appears in Levisham records early in the nineteenth century. John and Jane Morley brought five babies for christening between 1802 and 1809; then there is nothing more about them until we read their names in the Pauper

Book. John was getting parish help in the form of payments for leading turves throughout the period covered by the Pauper Book accounts (1828-52) with occasional cash hand-outs (*'relieved J.Morley 3s'*). Jane Morley and Margaret Gibb both died in 1834, their funerals paid for by the parish. Eight pounds of cheese (cost 4s 7d) was provided for Jane Morley's funeral, where Priscilla Jackson earned 1s 6d for *'waiting at funeral'*.

Most years, there was help given to one or more children in the village. There was a high birth rate – in a village with a population of one hundred and sixty eight in 1831, the number of christenings between 1820 and 1830 averaged five per year. Illegitimate babies were not uncommon. The 1834 accounts show weekly payments of 2s 6d to Priscilla Jackson *'for child'*, the child probably John, her unmarried daughter Mary's child. The following year a payment of 2s 6d was made *'to Rachel Stockill for child bearing;'* there is no christening entry to throw further light on this baby, but weekly payments continued annually for its maintenance. Jane Young appears in the book in 1832, an unmarried mother having the first of two illegitimate children. One shilling a week was paid for nine weeks for her lodgings, five shillings for the midwife, five pence for medicine, eight shillings a week for three weeks' 'lying in' then a weekly payment of 2s 6d for the child. This child, Martha, was by 1841 living with Priscilla Jackson – perhaps being fostered on behalf of the parish – and for her as for other poor children payments were made from time to time for shoes or clothes. Martha benefited from free schooling for seven years.

The facts and figures of an account book tell us nothing about the attitudes and feelings behind the transactions that are recorded, but the overall impression from reading through these accounts is of a community accepting responsibility for its impoverished members and treating them with humanity.

The possibilities of emigration must have been the subject of active discussion within the village, as in 1830 two families were given assistance by the parish to emigrate to Canada. The following year, four pounds was given to Richard Beecroft for his passage to America, a sum which would have paid his fare. The Yorkshire Gazette for the year 1830 advertised passages at three pounds on ships from Whitby to Quebec, *'the ship finding water and fuel'*, the passengers providing and cooking their own food on a journey likely to take about two months.

The expenses of the Morley and Garnet families were set out in the Overseers' Accounts in imperial currency:-

<u>March 31st 1830</u>

The Expenses of Two Families fitting them of for America viz J. Garnet his wife and 3 children D. Morley his wife and 2 children. From Whitby to Quebec

	£	s	d
2 sides of Bacon 9st 3lb at 5/6	2	10	8
3cwt 4st of Bread @ 22/6 per (?)	3	7	0
12st of flower 2/3 per stone	1	7	0
2 pecks of Oatmeal		3	4
Paid for Butter & Eggs		17	0
Do.	2	3	8
2 pecks of peas		4	0
to Beef		4	0
to Pottatoes 4 Bushels @ 2/6		10	0
to Candles 8lb at 6d		4	0
to Beef tubs		4	0
Tea 6lb	1	12	0
Coffee 6lb		10	0
Sugar 4st	1	8	0
Soap 4lb		2	6
1/4lb Peppers			8
Salt 1st			8
Cheese 18lb		7	6
Bread 16lb		6	8
Paid for the above Passage from Whitby to Quebec	17	0	0
What they are to have when they land at Quebec	5	0	0
	40	8	8
Balance		8	8
	40	0	0

The Levisham records do not name the ship the Morleys and Garnets sailed on, or give the date of sailing; it must have been during the financial year ending April 1830. There was no shortage of ships taking emigrants from Whitby to Quebec at that period – between April and June 1830 four ships, the *Addison,* the *Gunlare,* the *Jackson* and the *Earl Stanhope* all left for Quebec carrying over four hundred passengers looking for a new life in Canada.[6] One of the Overseers,

---

[6] Whitby Lit. and Phil.

Miles Close, claimed £1.15s for '*3 journeys to Whitby with J. Garnit & David Morley and their families to ship them to America*'. A further 14s was spent on '*spirits for J. Garnet & David Morley*', and 2s for '*a cobbel for J. Green to go to the ship on passing …*'. It sounds as if they were given a good send-off.

A reporter for the Yorkshire Gazette who witnessed emigrants setting off for Quebec from Hull on board the *Triton* in 1829 observed that '*they all seemed to evince an eagerness to quit the country of their birth, and judging from their countenances we should say that not 1 in 100 feels any regret on that score…*'. However, he recounted how one old woman was sea-sick as they set out, and thought they had perhaps reached 'Meriky' when she looked out and saw land, not realising that they were still in sight of harbour![7]

On arrival in Quebec, there would be a British Agent responsible for helping the immigrants. Some arrived in a destitute state, needing basic necessities of food and clothes. Others needed help in finding their contacts or friends. Those with no money would be offered labouring jobs on public works such as road-building from which they would hope to save up the money to buy land. There is no further information on these Levisham families once they had been seen off from Whitby. An attempt to trace them in Canada has so far only revealed that in the 1871 census for the Quebec province there were a number of families with the surnames Morley and Garnet, perhaps some of them of Levisham descent?

While emigration was an escape route for some, those who stayed had to face the rigours of the new Poor Law. In 1835, the Pickering Poor Law Union was set up covering a wide rural area that included Levisham. There were two Poorhouses already in existence, one at Undercliff in Pickering and a smaller house in Thornton Dale. The Guardians, under the Chairmanship of Colonel Thomas Mitchelson (a man with considerable local influence) held their first meeting at the Black Swan at 10am on Monday January 12th 1837. Reading their correspondence with the Poor Law Commissioners,[8] the impression emerges of a body of men not so much interested in

---

[7] Yorkshire Gazette April 28th 1829   [8] PRO

the problems of poverty as in keeping down costs and looking for opportunities to further their own interests – such as the appointment as Medical Officer of a young protegee of Col. Mitchelson at what some of his critics considered an inflated salary. The Guardians hoped initially to avoid having to build a new workhouse, not expecting many inmates, but the inconvenience of operating two houses made them decide to sell the old workhouses and build a new one in Pickering. It was built on Whitby Road in 1838 for a cost of £1231.2.6 and was from the first subject to criticism by the Inspectors, who took a similarly poor view of its management – *'the management appears to be on a par with the Architectural defects'*.[9]

A temporary stay by John Morley in 1841 is the only occasion discovered when a Levisham person needed to go to the workhouse. The Union granted outdoor relief[10] to Martha Young and John Jackson, both illegitimate children whose mothers are described as being 'in service in Levisham'. Meanwhile, the Levisham Overseers continued to maintain the two cottages, let the two gardens, and disburse small sums from the various charitable funds at their disposal. The cottages belonging to the Lockton Overseers of the Poor had fallen into dilapidation and were sold in 1859, the site to be developed for a school; the Levisham cottages were still in use in 1867[11] – when they were disposed of has not been discovered.

The acute poverty of the 1820's and 30's receded as village society adjusted itself to a style of farming needing fewer workers. At each census, the population was smaller, shrinking from 159 people in thirty households in 1841 to 108 people in twenty one households in 1891. The number who described themselves as 'farmer' remained almost the same (an increase from ten in 1841 to eleven in 1891), but agricultural labourers virtually disappeared. There were still a few living-in farm servants, and several of the farmers had sons working with them, but where in 1841 there had been eleven families dependent on a head of the household working as a farm labourer, in

---

[9] Report by Assistant Commissioner Hawley July 1842

[10] ie payments of money to those not in the workhouse

[11] listed in an Indenture. Percy Burnett papers, Whitby Lit. and Phil.

1891 there was only one. Farming had changed; other sources of employment such as the railway had arrived, and the poverty that was such a feature of the first half of the century had gone.

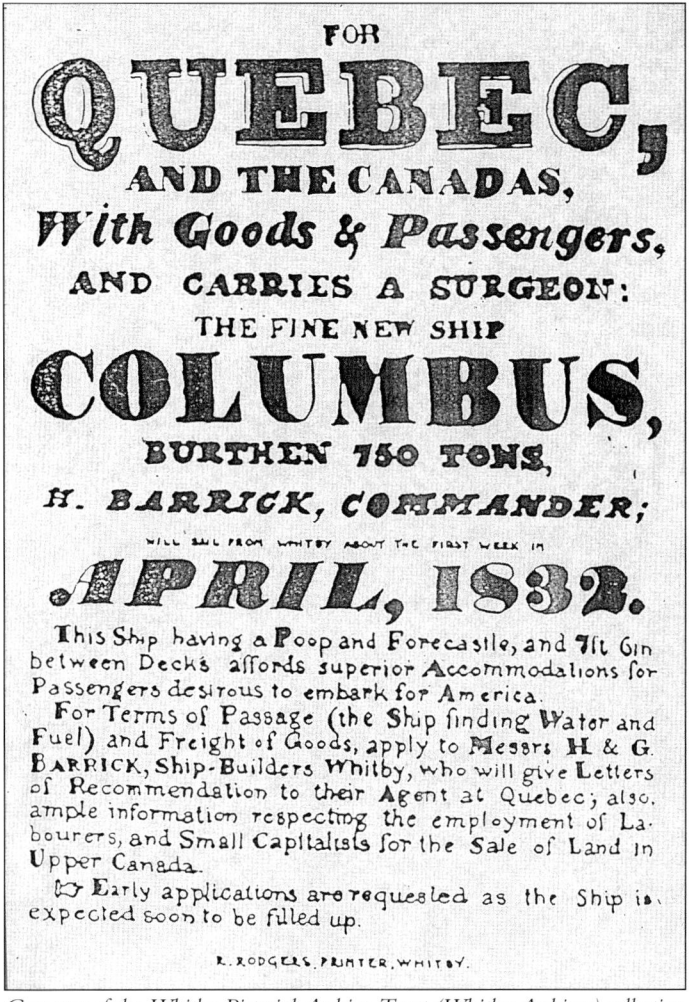

> **FOR QUEBEC, AND THE CANADAS,**
> **With Goods & Passengers,**
> AND CARRIES A SURGEON:
> THE FINE NEW SHIP
> **COLUMBUS,**
> BURTHEN 750 TONS,
> H. BARRICK, COMMANDER;
> WILL SAIL FROM WHITBY ABOUT THE FIRST WEEK IN
> **APRIL, 1832.**
>
> This Ship having a Poop and Forecastle, and 7ft 6in between Decks affords superior Accommodations for Passengers desirous to embark for America.
> For Terms of Passage (the Ship finding Water and Fuel) and Freight of Goods, apply to Messrs H & G. BARRICK, Ship-Builders Whitby, who will give Letters of Recommendation to their Agent at Quebec; also, ample information respecting the employment of Labourers, and Small Capitalists for the Sale of Land in Upper Canada.
> ☞ Early applications are requested as the Ship is expected soon to be filled up.
>
> R. RODGERS, PRINTER, WHITBY.

Courtesy of the Whitby Pictorial Archive Trust (Whitby Archives) collection

A Good Read

Diary of Robert Sharp of South Cave ed. Janice & Peter Crowther (OUP 1997)
Sharp was Schoolmaster and Parish Clerk of an East Riding village during the early the 19th century. His diary records all that was going on through the eyes of a shrewd and involved member of the community. He writes about a number of people who emigrated, looking for a better life in the New World – some made good, others did not.

Chapter 14:
Walker's Pit
a failed attempt at ironstone mining

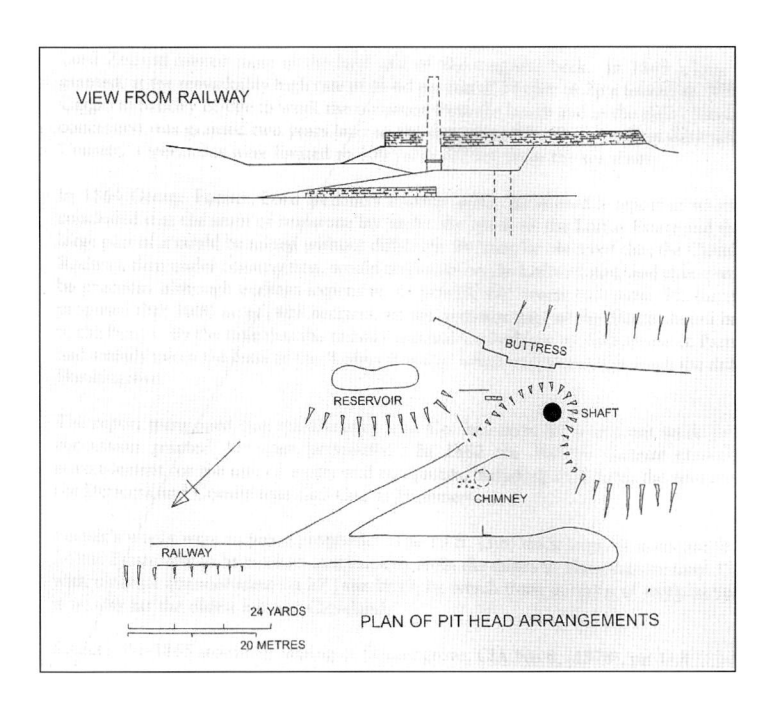

Sketches of Walker's Pit from Cleveland Ironstone: Memorial to John Owen.
by permission of The Cleveland Industrial Archaeological Society

CHRONOLOGY

Roman era	Iron workings on North York Moors
13C – 14C	Evidence of iron bloomery on Levisham Moor. Extensive iron working by monasteries.
16C-17C	Blast furnace at Rievaulx
early 18c	Technological advances eg. Abraham Darby at Coalbrookdale
1745	1st Darby-style blast furnace in the North (Co. Durham)
1837	1st Cleveland ironstone mine at Grosmont
1850's - 1926	Mining in Rosedale
1858	Shortlived Wreckhills mine and blast furnaces at Runswick Bay
1860-64	Mine and blast furnaces at Beck Hole, near Goathland
1862-69	Blast furnaces in Grosmont
1863-76	Glaisdale iron works: 3 blast furnaces
1859-66	Walker's Pit, Levisham

SOURCES

On the ground	Documentary
Remains of iron workings in Beck Hole, Glaisdale, Rosedale, Newtondale (Walker's Pit)	Published reminiscences by the Walker sisters
Tom Leonard Mining Museum, Skinningrove	Walker deeds (NYCRO)

Background

The discovery of how to produce iron was a significant landmark in human progress. Iron was used in Asia Minor over two thousand years ago, and had reached Britain by around 600 BC. People with iron technology had an immediate advantage over their neighbours: deadlier weapons, more productive agriculture.

During the medieval period, iron working was carried out at over one hundred sites in the area of the North York Moors; some monastic houses such as Rievaulx, and Guisborough developed and expanded the iron works they found on the lands under their control. Ironstone was collected from the places where outcrops of the ore-bearing seams of rock occurred. The stone was then mixed with charcoal and heated in small clay crucible-shaped furnaces or 'bloomeries' . The temperature was raised by hand or foot operated bellows to 1200°C – the point at which the waste material, the slag, melted and ran out of the furnace, leaving behind a malleable lump of iron, the 'bloom', which could be hammered into shape by the smith. The slag which was left lying around gives us an indication today of where these early iron forges were situated.

Advances were made in iron technology at Rievaulx: the monks harnessed water power to work the bellows in their bloomery, and after the dissolution of the monastery a blast furnace was developed in which the temperature could be raised to the point where the iron melted as well as the slag. The molten pig iron could be channelled into moulds, cast into its finished shape. The Rievaulx blast furnace continued in operation until 1643.

The iron industry received a new impetus in the eighteenth century. During the course of the Industrial Revolution, a combination of improved technology resulting from the work of innovators such as Abraham Darby (who used coke instead of charcoal to fire his furnaces), and ever-increasing demands from railway builders and expanding industries, provided the incentive for entrepreneurial characters to chance their arm by sinking pits to mine the ore, and to set up iron works to process it. The first coke-fired blast furnace in the north was opened in County Durham in 1745, fed with ironstone collected from the sea-shore between Saltburn and Scarborough. In 1800, the Tyne Iron Company opened in Newcastle, still relying on ore found on the coast, transported by sea.

The publication of William Smith's map in 1815 inaugurated the new science of geology, plotting the course of the different rock strata and so making it possible to predict where ironstone might be found under ground, rather than relying simply on stone exposed where the seams emerged on the surface. Geologists started looking for signs of iron-bearing seams of rock. A key date in the development of the iron industry in the North York Moors area was the year 1837: during the construction of the Whitby to Pickering Railway, a seam of ironstone was recognised in the walls of a tunnel being dug out near Grosmont.

Here was not only a source or ore, but, for the first time, a means of its transportation at hand! Geology and railways together opened up new possibilities.

For a period in the mid-nineteenth century, the north east of England was the biggest iron-producing area of the world. Middlesbrough, which saw the first commercial development of the Cleveland Main Seam became the fastest growing town in England. While iron-masters in Teeside and Tyneside were searching out new sources of supplies of ironstone, landowners in the rural area of the North York Moors realised that the iron underground could be of more value than all the crops or flocks on the surface. Ironstone was quarried from hillsides, brought out from drift mines, or reached by vertical shafts. Then came the expense of transporting this weighty material to the ironworks. It made sense to carry out some of the processing near to the mine. At Rosedale, where mining started on a small scale in 1856, calcining kilns were built in which the stone was baked to extract moisture, reducing its weight by up to 30% before it was carried away on the purpose-built railway that joined the main North York and Cleveland line at Battersby. At Grosmont and Glaisdale, blast furnaces to convert the ore into pig-iron were built near to the mines during the 1860s. The population of these small villages was suddenly swelled by an influx of miners; terraces of miners' cottages brought a new style of housing, industrial buildings changing the appearance of the landscape.

It was a precarious industry, offering the prospect of golden rewards to the owners and investors, but with dangers that were not always appreciated by the optimistic entrepreneurs, its future less certain than at first appeared. The industry was at its peak in the mid-nineteenth century. During the era of railway construction when the whole of England was overlaid by a network of iron rails, demand for iron seemed virtually unlimited. Wherever iron was discovered, a company would be formed to exploit it. Rosedale was transformed into a mining boom-town; blast furnaces were working in Grosmont by 1862 and in Glaisdale four years later. None of these ventures had a long life; small furnaces came and went, prospering for a time, closing down when times were bad, opening up again when trade looked up. In Rosedale, mining continued until 1927, but it was during the period of the 1860s and 1870s that it was at its height.

Some ambitious schemes had an even shorter life. The Victoria Iron and Cement Co. started operations in 1856 at Wreckhills, along the shore to the north of Runswick Bay, extracting ironstone from the cliffs and processing it in a calcining kiln and two blast furnaces. One night in March 1858 the night-watchman heard a rumbling noise; morning light revealed a land slip that had destroyed the whole £30,000 venture. Another company, the Whitby Iron Co. was started in 1858 by a Leeds businessman to extract and process the ironstone at Beck Hole, near Goathland. Two blast furnaces were built, an iron hoist, an engine house, three large boilers, a tall chimney, with ancillary buildings such as offices and store rooms, and a row of thirty three cottages for the workers.[1] The few working years of the mine were beset by problems – the unsatisfactory quality of the iron, structural faults in the building of the blast furnaces, and finally a land slip in 1864 that caused the abandonment of the works. Iron mining could be hugely profitable, but could end in disaster if undertaken without sufficient understanding of all the potential problems.

Levisham

Iron on Levisham Moor was worked from medieval times. The bloomery excavated in 1964 by the archaeologist Raymond Hayes, was thought at the time to be contemporary with the Iron Age settlement within which it was lying, but is now believed to date from the time when lords of the manor of Levisham paid 2s annually to the Exchequer for their iron forge. In the fourteenth century, John de Melsa had to fight a court case to establish the Lord of the Manor's right from 'time immemorial' to cut wood for making the charcoal needed for the furnace. In 1661, John Percey was still paying the 2s due for his iron works.

Nothing more is heard of Levisham iron until the middle of the nineteenth century. During this period of intensive activity in the

---

[1] P Wainwright: The Mines and Miners of Goathland, Beckhole & Greenend. Cleveland Mining Series 1996

development of the Cleveland iron industry a notice appeared in the Yorkshire Gazette advertising the sale of the Manor of Levisham.[2] 'There are', it said, '*extensive Beds of Iron Ore under the Commons and as the latter adjoin the Railway for 4 Miles, there is every facility for vending the Ore*'. The assignees of the Rev. Robert Skelton responsible for selling the estate to relieve his financial difficulties were here highlighting a feature likely to attract a buyer in the current economic climate.

The estate was bought by James Walker of Leeds, a successful businessman who had worked his way up through the family cloth-making firm (William Walker and Sons, later James Walker, finally Walker Brothers) started by his grandfather, a firm which won a medal for scarlet cloth at the Great Exhibition of 1851, where James Walker was involved in the preparations and was present at the opening ceremony. In their reminiscences of their father, his daughters depict him as an ambitious, enterprising character, involved in a variety of business ventures – just the sort of person who would be attracted by the prospects of profitable development of an up-and-coming industry. He was to be disappointed.

The Walker family had moved to Levisham Hall from Leeds by 1859. While his wife Elizabeth made the difficult adjustment to life away from her circle of city friends, accepting with good grace the role of lady of the manor – sending delicacies to the sick, running character-forming classes for young people, and while his children enjoyed the freedom of playing in the garden and exploring the countryside, James Walker began developing his iron works.

To finance the venture, Walker set about borrowing money: £2,000 at first in 1859 from Thomas Nunneley, surgeon, of Leeds, '*believing that Ironstone could be found…*'. But the initial explorations were unsuccessful and in 1861 he was seeking a further loan of £3,000 at 5% interest from Henry Hood (who had taken over Nunneley's investment), to enable him to continue.[3]

---

[2] Yorkshire Gazette January 19th 1856

[3] Papers relating to these financial transactions seen and quoted by John Owen, have not been traceable; but see NYCRO Deeds and Plans of Levisham Estate Micro. 2299/0460/Z825 and Register of Deeds IQ 124/185 and LA 44/85

His chosen site was on the east side of Newtondale, below Skelton Tower, south of Newton Dale Farm (later called Pit Farm). The track bed of the siding leading from the railway line to the mine workings can still be seen, and the top of the mine-shaft found amongst the undergrowth. A patch of rubble shows where the chimney stood before it was demolished in the 1960s, its stone used to fill in the shaft. There are traces of stone walling, some large stone blocks that may have been the engine beds, a hollowed out area that was probably a reservoir, but little else.

More information about the site can be learned from the sale advertisement published in September 1866.[4] Headed 'IRONSTONE AT LEVISHAM', it lists all that was to be included in the sale. There was the mine shaft:

'A Pit, 9 feet in diameter, walled 40 yards deep with ashlar stone and cement, and with 30 yards in depth of iron tubing, has been sunk ... It is about 96 yards deep...'

There was also mine machinery, comprising:

'...two engines (coupled) of 70-horse power, and two boilers with the necessary erections. They are all of the newest and best construction, and in working order...'

The advertisement speaks optimistically of the potential of the mine, the

'five or six seams of ironstone, which at the outcrops are from 4 to 12 feet thick each', and adds: *'there are, also, nodule seams from 1 to 2 feet thick each, and limestone, fire clay, and freestone exist in abundance.'*

The adjoining farm was envisaged as a potential site for blast furnaces, and it was noted that there was *'plenty of room for refuse slag'*.

Construction work on the mine buildings, using stone from the quarry in the hillside above, had been completed by 1865. According to the sale notice, the pit had been working for three months when it was put up for sale. The only information on what went wrong comes from Walker's daughter:

---

[4] Leeds Mercury September 29th 1866

> *'In the year 1866 there was much difficulty at my father's ironstone works. The breaking of machinery, water, and other mishaps caused delay and gave great anxiety to my father and mother.*
>
> *Much money was expended and years of hard work brought no return, and in the end the pit had to be closed down, and we left Levisham.'*

The Walker family's time in Levisham is recorded in Census Returns, Parish Registers, churchyard monuments. The 1861 census shows them living at the Hall, James and Elizabeth with their six children, three girls and three boys, ranging in age from nine years to six months. Another daughter born the next year died at 3 months. Perhaps the stress and anxiety over the pit failure contributed to death of Elizabeth in 1867 at the age of 39 soon after the birth of her last daughter who lived for only ten weeks. James and the children returned to Leeds, where in spite of the train of misfortunes that overshadowed their time in Levisham the girls retained an affection for the village that brought them back on visits until 1938.[5]

The estate took some time to sell. The mine was never worked again. It was the shooting rights on the moor that eventually attracted buyers, the rich variety of the landscape leading into another development in the history of the village.

A Good Read

The Map that changed the the World Simon Winchester (Viking 2001)
An account of the remarkable life of William Smith, who made the first map of the geology of England, and grasped the significance of being able to predict where different strata of rock would be found.

[5] Church Visitors' Book.

Bibliography

Abbreviations

VCR	Victoria County History
NRR	North Riding Records
NYCRO	North Yorkshire County Record Office
Borth	Borthwick Institute of Historical Research
PRO	Public Record Office
YAS	Yorkshire Archaeological Society
Whitby Lit. & Phil.	Whitby Literary & Philosophical Society
YAJ	Yorkshire Archaeological Journal
LVA	Levisham Village Archive

Primary Sources

Census Returns	PRO; County Library (transcript LVA)
Church records: Terriers, Visitations, Court Books	Borth.
Enclosure Award	NYCRO (transcript LVA)
George Dixon's school books	Photo copy LVA
Hearth Tax Returns	PRO
Levisham Manor Court Book (19th century)	NYCRO
Levisham Poor Book 1829-1924	NYCRO (transcript LVA)
Malton Cartul\ary (transcript LVA)	BM Cotton MS Claudius DXI. Microfilm Borth.
Muster Rolls	PRO
Parish Registers	NYCRO (transcript LVA)
Percy Burnett's Papers	Whitby Lit. & Phil.
Poor Law Correspondence 1851-76	PRO (MH 12/14575-1458)
Register of Deeds	NYCRO
Religious Census 1851	PRO (HO 129 530)
School History Sheet 1900- 1915; correspondence	PRO (Ed 21/19525; 21/64239; 49/185)
Tithe Map and Schedule Copy	LVA
Valuation 1910	NYCRO (transcript LVA)
Vestry Minutes 1794-1847	NYCRO PR/Lev 3
Wills	Borth. (calendared LVA)

Printed Primary Sources

Atkinson Rev.J.C. ed	Quarter Sessions	North Riding Record Soc.	1884
Atkinson, Rev.J.C.	Forty Years in a Moorland Parish	M.T.D.Rigg pub.	1992
Bede ed. McClure & Collins	Ecclesiastical History of the English People	O.U.P.	1999
Brown, W (ed)	Yorks Inquisitions	YAS Record12	1891
Brown, W (ed)	Yorks Lay Subsidy 1301	YAS Record 21	1896
Calendars of Inquisitions Post Mortem			
Chantry Certificates	Surtees Society vos 1 & 2		1892
Clay, J.W. (ed)	Suppression Papers	YAS Record 48	1912

Committee of Council of Education : Inspector's Reports			
Cross, C & Vickers, N	Monks, Friars & Nuns in 16C Yorkshire	YAS Record Series vol. CL	1995
English, B. (ed)	Yorkshire Hundred & Quo Warranto Rolls	YAS Record Series CLI	1996
Faull, M.	Domesday Book : Yorkshire		1986
Ollard, S.L. & Walker, P.C.	Archbishop Herring's Visitation Returns	YA S Record Series LXXI-LXXIX	1929
	Report of Select Committee of Agriculture		
Marshall W.	Rural Economy of Yorkshire		1788
Trade Directories			
Turton, R.B.	North Riding Records, New Series 4 vols.		1894
Walker, H., J., B.M.	Recollections	Leeds	1930
Walker, B.M.	The Well of Life	Leeds	1939

Pamphlets, articles

Green, Harry	Manor of Fyling Court Leet	Private paper, in Whitby Lit. and Phil	2000
Allerston, Pamela	English Village Development	Instno.Institute of British Geographers Transactions & Papers no.81	1969
Atherden, M.A.	Late Quaternary Vegetational History of the N.York Moors	Journal of Biogeography	1976
Barker, R.	The Small Print of History	Local Historian vol.15 no 8	1983
Bishop, T. A. M.	Monastic Granges in Yorkshire	English Historical Review	1936
Hall, R.A. & Lang, J.T.	St Mary's Church, Levisham	YAJ vol.58	1986
Halse, B.	Population Mobility in the village of Levisham 1541-1900	Local Population Studies no.65	2000
Hayes, R.H.		N.E.Yorkshire Studies	
Moorhouse, S.	Medieval Monastic Farm on Levisham Moor	CBA Forum	1986
Moorhouse, S.	Monastic Estates	Br. Archaeological Ass. Report 203	1989
Rahtz, P.A. & Watts, L.	Excavations in Ryedale 2000	Ryedale Historian no.21	2002
Rievaulx Abbey	Experimental Archaeology leaflet	English Heritage	
Roberts, B.K.	Back Lanes and Tofts	Architectural & Archaeological Soc. of Durham & N'umberland	1990

Books
General

	Victoria County History: North Riding, & Vol III: Ecclesiastical History		
Hey, David (ed)	Oxford Companion to Local & Family History	Oxford	2002
Richardson, John	Local Historian's Encyclopedia	Historical Publications	1986
Stephens, W.B.	Sources for English Local History	Phillimore	1994
Tate, W.E.	The Parish Chest	CUP	1960
Tiller, Kate	English Local History: an introduction	Alan Sutton	1992

Introduction

Emmison, F.G.	Archives and Local History	Methuen	1966
Finberg, H.P.R.	The Local Historian and His Theme	Leicester U P	1952
Finberg, H.R. P. & Tripp,V. H. T.	Local History: Objective and Pursuit	David & Charles	1973
Hoskins , W.G.	Local History in England	Longman	1972

| Hoskins, W.G. | English Local History: Past & Future | Leicester UP | 1966 |
| Phythian-Adams, C. | Re-thinking English Local History | Leicester U P | 1987 |

Chapter 1

Aston, M	Interpreting the Landscape	Batsford	1985
Baker, A.R.H. & Harley, J.B. (ed)	Man Made the Land	David & Charles	1973
Belcher, H	Scenery of the Whitby and Pickering Railway	EP Publishing Ltd	1976
Breakell, W.	Old Pannier Tracks	N Y Moors National Park	1987
Hoskins, W.G.	Making of the English Landscape	Penguin	1991
Macmahon, K.A.	Roads and Turnpike trusts in East Yorkshire	E.Yorks. Local History Soc.	1964
Moore, R.F.	Lime Roads in the Whitby District	Whitby Lit.& Phil.	1972
Potter, G.W.J.	History of the Whitby and Pickering Railway	London	1906 (1969)
Spratt, D.A. & Harrison .J.D.(ed)	The North York Moors Landscape Heritage	N Y Moors National Park	1989
Sewell, Joseph T.	Medieval Roads	Whitby Lit. & Phil.	1971
Tomlinson, W.W.	The North Eastern Railway	Newcastle	1914

Chapter 2

Hayes, R. (ed)	Levisham Moor. Archaeological Investigations 1957-1978	N.Y. Moors National Park & Scarborough Archaeological & Historical Soc.	1983
Spratt, D.A. (ed)	Prehistoric and Roman Archaeology of North-East Yorkshire	Co. for British Archaeology	1993
Vyner, B.E. (ed)	Moorland Monuments	CBA Report 101	1995

Chapter 3

Chibnall, Marjorie	Anglo-Norman England	Blackwell	1986
Darby, H.C. & Maxwell, I.S.	Domesday Geography of Northern England	Cambridge	1978
Mills, A. D.	Dictionary of English Place Names	Oxford	1998
Morris, R.W.	Yorkshire through Place Names	David and Charles	1982
Stenton, F. M.	Anglo-Saxon England	Oxford	1989

Chapters 4 and 5

Faull, M.L. & Stinson, M. (ed)	Domesday Book: Yorkshire	Phillimore	1986
Finn R W	Domesday Book: A Guide	Phillimore	1973
Grant Raymond	The Royal Forests of England	Alan Sutton	1991
McLynn Frank	1066: The Year of the Three Battles	Jonathan Cape	1998
Miller E. & Hatcher J.	Medieval England: Rural Society & Economic Change	Longman	1978
Owen, Dorothy M.	Church and Society in Medieval Lincolnshire	History of Lincolnshire	1981
Powick M.	The Thirteenth Century	Oxford	
Titow, J.Z.	English Rural Society	Allen & Unwin	1969

Chapter 6

Burton, Janet	The Monastic Order in Yorkshire 1069-1215	CUP	1994
Golding, Brian	Gilbert of Sempringham and the Gilbertine Order	Oxford	1995
Knowles, David	Monastic Orders in England	Cambridge	1963
Platt, C	The Monastic Grange in Medieval England	London	1969

Richardson, H.G.	English Jewry under Angevin Kings	Methues	1960
Waites, Bryan	Moorland and Vale-land Farming in N.E.England	Borthwick Paper 32	1967
Waites, Bryan	Monasteries and Landscapes in N.E.England	Multum in Parvo Press	1997

Chapter 7

Godfrey, John	The English Parish 600-1300	SPCK	1969
Swanson, R N	Church and Society in Late Medieval England	Blackwell	1989
Frank, I W	History of the Medieval Church	SCM	1995
Tate, W.E.	The Parish Chest	CUP	1960

Chapters 9 - 12

Clay, J.W.(ed.)	Dugdale's Visitation of Yorkshire	Exeter	1917
Goody, J. Thirsk, J. Thompson, E.P. (ed)	Family and Inheritance	CUP	1976
Heal, Felicity & Holmes, Clive	The Gentry in England & Wales 1500-1700	Macmillan	1994
Mercer, E.	English Vernacular Architecture Houses of the North York Moors		1975
Strong, Ruth	Methodism in a Moorland Village	Blacksmith House Pub.	1999

Chapter 13

Crowther, Janice E. & Peter E.(ed)	Diary of Robert Sharp of South Cave	Records of Social & Economic History New Series 26 OUP	1997
Erickson, C	Leaving England: Essays on British Emigration in the 19th Century	London	1944

Chapter 14

Chapman, Keith	Cleveland Ironstone Industry and its impact on Teesside	Industrial Archaeology of Cleveland	1997
Hempstead, C.A.(ed.)	Cleveland Iron and Steel	British Steel Corporation	1979
Owen, John S.	Cleveland Ironstone Mining	Tom Leonard Mining Museum	1995
Wainwright, Peter	The Mines and Miners of Goathland, Beckhole and Greenend	Industrial Archaeology of Cleveland	1996
Winchester, Simon	The Map that Changed the World Cleveland Ironstone: Memorial to John Own	Viking Cleveland Industrial Arch. Soc./North York Moors National Park	2001

Glossary

affeeror	official of a manorial court, responsible for assessing penalties
assart	enclosure taken from forest land
aumbrie	cupboard
benefice	a church living; unbeneficed: clergy who did not have charge of a parish
bilman	one who fought with a bill or halbert, a weapon combining an axe-blade and spear on a pole
bloomery	furnace in which iron ore is heated to the point where the slag melts, leaving a residue of malleable iron
bovate/oxgang	measure of land based on what one ox could plough in a year
canon	
cartulary	collection of charters
carucate	measure of land: amount that could be ploughed in a year by team of eight oxen
cess	tax or rate
chapel of ease	church built where the parish church is some distance from the population
chapelry	section of a parish served by a chapel-of-ease
churching	church service for a woman following childbirth
close	enclosed piece of land
curate	(old usage) a clergyman, someone with the care or 'cure' of souls
demesne	land that retained by Lord of the Manor for his own use, worked on his behalf by his tenants
doublet	close-fitting man's jacket
dubler	dish, often pewter
feudalism	system of tenure under which land was held from a lord, and ultimately from the king, in return for a variety of services
glebe	land belonging to the church
grange	outlying monastic farm (literally, barn or granary)
hagg	woodland
halbert (or halberd)	see bilman
ing	pasture by a stream
inquisition	a judicial enquiry; / i. post mortem: enquiry into possessions of tenant of the crown after his death
kimlin	wooden trough for kneading dough, etc.
manor	unit of land-holding held by a lord, ultimately from the crown
mark	unit of currency worth two thirds of a pound
minster	church served by a community of priests, before parish system
outlaw	one who failed to appear in court to answer charges, so declared outside protection of law
pauper	destitute person, requiring charitable help
pig iron	iron produced by heating to a temperature when the iron melts and can be run off into a mould
reckon	(various spellings) iron bar hanging in chimney on which cooking pots were hung
rector	person with responsibility for a parish, entitled to tithes; originally the incumbent, but rectory could be given to a monastery and after Reformation to a layman.
rectory	office of rector; later, word used for rector's house
recusant	one who refused to follow legal requirement to attend parish church; usually Roman Catholic
regarder	Forest official
reeve	overseer acting on behalf of lord of the manor
sallet	helmet
starr	contract made between Jews and Christians (term used before 1290, when Jews expelled from England)
terrier	inventory of land
tithe	tax of tenth of all produce payable to the Church
toft	piece of land between house and back lane in planned village
verderer	officer of the Forest Courts

vert	forest vegetation, protected under Forest Law
Vestry	meeting of parish officials which in 16th and 17th centuries took over some functions of manor court
vicar, vicarage	deputy for a rector, appointed as incumbent of parish when the rectory had been given to a monastery
vill	village, township
Visitation (episcopal)	examination of the state of the diocese by the bishop
wain(e)	wagon
wether	castrated ram
woodward	officer appointed to look after forest by landowner

Index

Adamson	81, 87, 91,132	canals	8, 10, 14
advowson	97, 108, 110	Cartulary	40, 60, 63, 64
affeerors	36	carucate	39, 90
agister	52	castles	10, 37, 78
Agriculture, Committee on	112, 129	census	3, 4, 86, 96, 106, 107, 114, 116, 120
Allanson	119		121, 122, 128, 132, 135, 136, 146
Allerston	39, 99, 100, 121	cess	130
alum	16	chantry	73
America	108, 128, 129, 130, 133, 135	Chapel, Chapelry	64, 74, 82, 96, 98, 99, 102,
Anglo-Saxon	8, 25, 26, 27, 28, 29, 30, 44		103, 119
Appleton le Street	117, 118	charcoal	11, 46, 54, 141, 143
archaeology	2, 21, 24	Charity Wood	131
archer	90	Church of England	97, 98, 99, 118
assart	52, 55	churchwarden	74, 78, 81, 82, 87, 92, 96, 119, 123
Atkinson, Canon	100	Cistercian	60, 61, 62, 63
Ayton	50	Clarke	89
Bayley	81, 89	clerk	29, 34, 54, 68, 69, 71, 121, 130
Baysdale	60, 63	Cleveland	139, 140, 142, 144
Beck Hole	16, 17, 140, 143	Close, Miles	112, 135
Bede	26, 27, 29, 31	Collinson	98
Beecroft	133	Conquest, Norman	27, 29, 30, 31, 32, 33, 36,
Bel, Robert le	44, 63		37, 46, 50, 60, 65
Benedictine	52, 53, 62	Consett	54, 87, 89
Berry, William	122, 123, 125	constable	54, 77, 78, 79, 80, 81, 82
Bigod	40, 44, 46, 52	Corn Laws	128, 129
billman	??????	Court Leet	36, 43, 44, 78
Black Death	34, 37, 39	Craike	109
Blansby Park	23, 50, 56	Cropton	99, 102, 117
blast furnace	140, 141, 142, 143, 145	Crosley, William	15
bloomery	23, 140, 141, 143	Crosscliffe	109
Bolebec, Ralph, Osbert, Hugh	39, 40, 41, 42, 43,	crosses Malo, Lilla, Mauley	13
	44, 45, 46, 52, 53, 60, 63, 64, 65, 66, 70	curate	65, 69, 72, 97, 98, 99, 100, 102
Borthwick Institute	84, 87, 96, 97	Darby, Abraham	140, 141
Botham, Henry	72	Darrell	87, 88
bovate	44, 45	Deeds, Register of	101, 102, 106, 110, 111, 132
bowmen	56	Dickinson	92, 93
Boynton	117	Directory	120, 121
Braygate	13, 90, 108	Dissolution of the Monasteries	73, 141
Bronze Age	8, 11, 12, 23	Dixon	114, 119, 122
burial mounds	23, 24	Dobson	79, 85, 90
Burnet, Philip	113, 136	Domesday Book	4, 22, 23, 26, 27, 34, 37, 39, 41, 42
Burniston	109	Duncomb	131
Canada	129, 133, 134, 135	Dundale	41, 42, 46, 63, 64, 66

Durham	71, 140, 141	husbandman	85, 86
Ebberston	79, 86, 99, 100, 101, 110	Inquisition Post Mortem	45, 70
education	68, 110, 111, 116, 117, 118, 123, 131	inspectors	116, 118, 128, 136
Education, Committee of Council for	116, 118, 119	inventory	89, 91, 93
Education, Department of	116, 120, 123, 125	iron	11, 12, 17, 23, 24, 30, 44, 46, 54, 57, 90, 92, 93, 140, 141, 142, 143, 144, 145, 146
Ellis, John	119	Iron Age	6, 20, 22, 23, 30, 143
emigration	128, 129, 130, 133, 135	ironstone	139, 140, 141, 142, 143, 144, 145, 146
Enclosure(s)	3, 8, 20, 23, 42, 55, 61, 81, 86, 100, 101, 105, 106, 107, 108, 110, 111, 112, 113, 114	Jackson	119, 132, 133, 134, 136
Fairweather	72, 87	Jews	65
farmer	9, 11, 16, 23, 30, 82, 85, 91, 93, 100, 103, 107, 111, 113, 114, 119, 120, 121, 129, 130, 136	Judson, Richard	73, 74, 77, 80, 81
		jury	44, 45, 64, 79
Farwath	23	Justices of the Peace	78, 79
Fen Bog	16, 17	Keldholme	60, 62, 63
Forest (of Pickering)	50, 51, 52, 53, 55, 56, 57	Kidstye	87
Forest Eyre	49, 52	King, Edna and Derek	21
Forest Law	49, 50, 51, 54, 57	King Street	13
forester	40, 52, 53, 54, 56	Kirby Grindalyth	99
Foulbridge	14, 62	Kirby Misperton	121
Frankpledge, View of	44, 45	Kirkbymoorside	110
Fulstow	40, 45, 65, 66	Kirkham	62
Gallows Dyke	44	Knights Templar	14, 62
Garnet	134, 135	labourer	63, 80, 85, 90, 101, 110, 113, 114, 128, 129, 130, 131, 132, 136
Gates, Sir Henry	91	landscape	7, 8, 9, 11, 15, 17, 20, 21, 60, 107, 113, 142, 146
gentleman	79, 85, 86, 100, 102, 104, 108, 109, 110, 119, 122	Land Tax	82, 106, 113
Gibb	119, 131, 132, 133	Lastingham	26, 31, 41, 132
Gilbertines	62, 66	Lay Subsidy	66, 68, 71
glebe	69, 74, 102, 103	Levisham Hall	101, 112, 114, 144
Glebe Farm	112	Levisham Moor	17, 21, 22, 23, 30, 44, 59, 60, 104, 140, 143
Goathland	16, 17, 62, 79, 109, 117, 140, 143		
Godfrey de Melsa	4	Lightowler, Henry	120, 121, 122
grange	10, 35, 46, 60, 63, 64, 66	lime	13, 16, 98, 113
Grange Farm	112	Limpseygate	13, 90, 108, 111
Green Cottage	105, 112	Lindisfarne	26, 28, 29
Green, John	113, 135	Little Field	90, 108
Greystock, Ralph	108, 109	Low Grange	112
Grosmont	16, 17, 62, 140, 141, 142	Lowstead Farm	114
Grove House	104, 112	Lumley, Lady	117
Guardians, Board of	128, 130	Magee, Miss	125
Hackness	13, 62	Malton	14, 40, 41, 42, 45, 46, 60, 62, 63, 64, 65, 66, 79, 88, 99, 102, 117, 128
Harald Hardrada	36		
Harding	100, 101, 108, 109, 110, 113, 114	manor	35, 36, 38, 39, 40, 43, 44, 46, 54, 63, 71, 78, 86, 91, 101, 103, 104, 108, 109, 110, 114, 120, 122, 143, 144
Harlan	119		
Harold	35, 36	Manor House	43, 112, 120, 122
harrying of the north	4, 34, 37, 39, 62	Marishes	88, 100, 109
Hearth Tax	75, 77, 80, 81, 82, 84, 86, 92	Marshall	106, 111
Helmsley	37, 49, 62, 79, 88	Medical Officer	136
Herring, Archbishop	96, 99, 116, 117, 118	Melsa, Geoffrey, John, Scholastica	4, 54, 143
Hewitson	87, 89	Merry, Robert	112, 130
Hicks, George	74	Methodist, Methodism	74, 96, 97, 98, 100, 103
Hoggshagh	45	Middlesbrough	142
Hole of Horcum	44	Middleton	31, 73, 74, 99, 101, 102, 103
Holgate, Archbishop	117	mill, miller	44, 45, 46, 53, 64, 66, 81, 85, 100, 103, 114, 120
Homestead House	112		
Horseshoe Inn	121	mine, mining	16, 17, 139, 140, 141, 142, 143, 144, 145, 146
Howe Bridge	14, 66, 79		
Hudson, George	17	minster	29, 32
Hull	130, 135		
hungeld	51		

Index

Mitchell	79, 91
Mitchelson	131, 135, 136
monastery	26, 27, 29, 60, 63, 69, 141
Morcar	34, 36, 38, 39
Morley	119, 132, 133, 134, 135, 136
Muster Roll	84, 90
Ness Head	56
Newton House Farm	112
Newtondale	8, 12, 15, 16, 53, 55, 56, 71, 87, 89, 91, 93, 101, 104, 112, 131, 132, 140, 145
Norden	55
Normanby	117, 119
Northumbria	13, 26, 28, 29, 32, 35, 36, 38, 70
Nunnington	117
Oates, Anthony	101, 110, 112
Old Wives Way	13
outlaw	35, 53
Overseers of the Poor	78, 79, 82, 87, 104, 119, 128, 130, 131, 132, 134, 136
oxgang	86, 90, 92, 93, 100
pannierway	?????
parish	2, 3, 4, 10, 11, 13, 29, 31, 44, 60, 63, 68, 69, 70, 71, 72, 73, 74, 78, 79, 80, 82, 87, 92, 97, 98, 99, 100, 102, 103, 108, 110, 116, 117, 118, 119, 121, 123, 128, 129, 130, 131, 132, 133
Parish Clerk	121, 130, 137
Parish Registers	3, 4, 81, 84, 87, 88, 92, 98, 100, 101, 106, 110, 131, 146
Parsonage House	98, 101, 103
Pa(i)te	80, 91, 92, 93
Pickering	8, 11, 13, 14, 15, 16, 17, 23, 30, 31, 34, 36, 37, 38, 39, 44, 46, 49, 50, 52, 53, 54, 55, 56, 57, 66, 70, 72, 73, 79, 82, 88, 90, 96, 98, 101, 102, 109, 110, 135, 136, 141
Pilgrimage of Grace	68, 74
pluralism	97, 99
poaching	54, 71, 73
Poad	85, 86, 87, 93, 101, 103, 108, 109, 110, 119, 120, 123, 125, 131
Poll Tax	39
Poor Book	104, 110, 128
Poor Law	78, 128, 130, 135
Poor, Overseers of	78, 79, 82, 87, 104, 119, 128, 130, 131, 132, 134, 136
Postgate	88
Prestman	90
Priory, Prior (of Malton)	40, 41, 42, 45, 46, 60, 62, 63, 64, 65, 66
Quebec	130, 134, 135
railway	8, 11, 16, 17, 18, 104, 112, 132, 137, 141, 142, 144, 145
rector	15, 44, 54, 69, 70, 71, 73, 74, 75, 98, 99, 100, 101, 102, 103, 104, 108, 109, 110, 112, 114, 122, 123, 131
Read, (Rede, Reed)	72, 87, 88, 89, 109
Reformation	68, 70, 72, 73, 74, 84
regarder	50, 52
Rhumbard Snout	22, 23
Rievaulx	60, 62, 140, 141
Road Surveyors	80, 82
roads	6, 9, 10, 11, 14, 41, 79, 106, 109, 111, 113
Rolle, Richard	71, 72
Roman	8, 10, 23, 26, 27, 28, 29, 30, 140
Rosedale	50, 60, 62, 63, 101, 102, 103, 140, 142, 143
Rowle	72
Ryedale	26, 31, 84, 117
salt	13, 44, 56, 65, 134
Saltburn	141
Saltergate	13, 53
Salton	118
Scagglethorpe	120
school	31, 73, 82, 99, 103, 115, 116, 117, 118, 119, 120, 121, 122, 123, 125, 132, 133, 136
School Board	116, 118, 123, 125
Seven, River	38, 50
Sharp, Robert	130, 137
sheriff	55, 56, 79
Simpson	119
Sinnington	31, 101, 117
Skelton	15, 95, 98, 101, 102, 103, 104, 112, 114, 120, 122, 131, 144, 145
Skinningrove	140
Sleights Road	13
Smith, William	141, 146
South Cave	130, 137
Speenhamland	128, 129
St Mary's Church	13, 33, 34, 60, 67, 72, 95, 96, 102
Stamford Bridge	28, 34, 35, 36
Standard, Battle of	13, 34
Starr	65
Stead	103, 120
Stephenson, George	16
Stockill	119, 131, 133
Stone Age	21
Stor(e)y	54, 71, 88, 89, 90
Tate	119
Terriers	74, 96, 98, 102, 120, 132
Thornton Dale	71, 98, 117, 135
tithe	3, 8, 42, 69, 72, 82, 87, 100, 101, 103, 106, 109, 110, 113, 114
Tostig	35, 36
trod	12, 13
Tuke	14, 87, 90, 106, 111
turves	132, 133
Tyne Iron Company	141
Unions (Poor Law)	130
Valor Ecclesiasticus	68, 70
vert	50, 54
verderer	50, 52
Vestry	78, 82, 116, 119
vicar	69, 73, 98, 99
Viking	26, 28, 32, 146
Visitation	68, 74, 96, 97, 99, 101, 116, 117, 118
Walker	17, 72, 139, 140, 144, 145, 146
Wallis	119
Walmsley	113
wapentake	28, 90
War Camp	23
Ward	119
Watkins, Rev. F.	121, 122
Watson	54, 55, 67, 72, 73, 131

Whitby 8, 13, 14, 15, 16, 17, 18, 26, 27, 29, 31, 60, 61, 62, 72, 73, 88, 127, 134, 135, 136, 137, 141, 143
Wilberforce 130
Wilkinson 79, 88, 90
will 68, 69, 71, 72, 73, 81, 84, 85, 86, 87, 88, 89, 90, 91, 92, 101, 119, 131, 132
Wilton 109
Wimbush, Barnes 17
Woodcock 113
woodward 52, 53
workhouse 128, 130, 136
Wreckhills 140, 143
Wykeham 60, 62, 63
Yedingham 14, 62
yeoman 54, 79, 83, 84, 85, 86, 93, 101, 109, 110, 132
York 17, 21, 26, 36, 38, 45, 55, 56, 65, 66, 70, 72, 84, 97, 98, 99, 100, 110
Young 132, 133, 136